P9-DBX-958

HOW TO ATTRACT BIRDS

Created and designed by
the editorial staff of ORTHO BOOKS

Project editor	**Ken Burke**
Editor	Jessie Wood
Writer	Michael McKinley
Designer	James Stockton

Ortho Books

Publisher
Robert L. Iacopi

Editorial Director
Min S. Yee

Managing Editors
Anne Coolman
Michael D. Smith
Sally W. Smith

Production Manager
Ernie S. Tasaki

Editors
Jim Beley
Susan Lammers
Deni Stein

Design Coordinator
Darcie S. Furlan

System Managers
Christopher Banks
Mark Zielinski

Photographic Director
Alan Copeland

Photographers
Laurie A. Black
Richard A. Christman

Production Editors
Linda Bouchard
Alice Mace
Kate O'Keeffe

Asst. System Manager
William F. Yusavage

Chief Copy Editor
Rebecca Pepper

Photo Editors
Anne Dickson-Pederson
Pam Peirce

National Sales Manager
Garry P. Wellman

Sales Associate
Susan B. Boyle

Operations Director
William T. Pletcher

Operations Assistant
Gail L. Davis

Administrative Assistant
Georgiann Wright

Address all inquiries to
Ortho Books
Chevron Chemical Company
Consumer Products Division
575 Market Street
San Francisco, CA 94105

Chevron

Chevron Chemical Company
575 Market Street, San Francisco, CA 94105

Front Cover:
Thase Daniel, Bruce Coleman Inc.
Male Northern Cardinal on flowering
crab apple.

Back cover:
Stephen J. Krasemann, Peter Arnold Inc.
Evening Grosbeaks feeding on
sunflower seeds.

Title page:
Gregory Scott, Photo Researchers, Inc.
Blue Jays often bury food under soil or
snow, and retrieve it later.

Consultants:
Stephen F. Bailey, Ph.D.
Museum of Vertebrate Zoology
University of California at Berkeley
Berkeley, CA

Roger Harris, M.S.
Mill Valley, CA

Charles R. Smith, Ph.D.
Director of Public Education
Laboratory of Ornithology
Cornell University
Ithaca, NY

Acknowledgments:
Typography by Turner & Brown,
Santa Rosa, CA

Color separations by Color Tech,
Redwood City, CA

Copy editing and proofreading by
editcetera, Berkeley, CA

Illustrations:
Cyndie Clark-Huegel
Wayne Clark

Photography:
Photographers are listed by photo
agency. Names of photographers are
followed by page numbers on which
their work appears. R = right, L = left,
C = center, T = top, B = bottom.

Animals Animals
Ken Carmichael 88TR
M.A. Chappel 92C
Margot Conte 67L
Michael Habicht 63BR
Conrad J. Kitsz 12T
Z. Leszczynski 66L
James E. Lloyd 3BCL, 22
Willard Luce 19
Bruce A. Macdonald 35TR, 57, 76L
Patti Murray 18TL, 49
Alan Rokach 14BR
Leonard Rue, Jr. 66R
Leonard Lee Rue III 24TL
J.C. Stevenson 12B
Lynn M. Stone 51R
Marty Stouffer 3TL, 4
John Trott 17BR, 50TL, 52
Fred E. Unverhau 17TR
Tom Vanderschmidt 47
Fred Whitehead 16
Jack Wilburn 28CR
Ron Willocks 84C
Dale and Marian Zimmerman 30BL
Leonard Zorn 14TC

Peter J. Arnold, Inc.
Stephen J. Krasemann 81R, 93L
John R. MacGregor 68C

Herbert C. Clark: 24TC, 76BR, 77L,
78R, 82L, 88L, 88BR

Bruce Coleman Inc.
Fred J. Alsop III 79L
J.D. Bartlett 86BL
Bob and Clara Calhoun 69L
Robert P. Carr 7, 75R
Thase Daniel 80L
Wayne Lankinen 91BR
Laura Riley 3BR, 38TL, 82R
John Shaw 11B, 85TL
Glenn Short 37
Joseph Van Wormer 6B
L. West 76R

Cornell Laboratory of Ornithology
L.M. Bartlett 59BL
L.B. Chapman 79TR
Bill E. Duyck 81L
Michael Hopiak 42, 68R
Uve F. Hublitz 13TL, 59CL
Morgan Jones 58TC
S. Otis 39B
O.F. Soule 72BR

DRK Photo
Wayne Lankinen 90L

Stephen J. Krasemann 24TR, 74C,
77R

Grant Heilman
George H. Harrison 63C
Hal Harrison 85R
Barry L. Runk 6T, 39TL

Michael McKinley 26, 30CL

Ortho Books
Josephine Coatsworth 28BC

Photri
Sam Blakesley 94
Robert Dunning 91TR
Leonard Lee Rue III 71R, 75L, 87L

Photo Researchers, Inc.
Peter Aitken 72TR
Bob and Elsie Boggs 89R
John Bova 40TR, 93R
John M. Burnley 70R
Stephen Dalton 3TCL, 8
Kent and Donna Dannen 40C
Joe DiStefano 35BR
Bill Dyer 9, 80R, 86R
Patrick Grace 3BL, 36
J.A. Hancock 79BR
Olen S. Hanson 3TR, 48
Russ Kinne 5
George Leavens 38RC
Pat and Tom Leeson 74R
Alexander Lowry 51L
Thomas W. Martin 58TR,89C
Steve Maslowski 27BC, 27BR, 31
Anthony Mercieca 66C, 74L
James F. Parnell 18TC
O.S. Pettingill 34CL, 84R
Rod Planck 28BR, 90R
J.H. Robinson 63BL
Leonard Lee Rue III 70L, 86TL
Delbert Rust 87R
Gregory Scott 3BR, 13TR, 64, 90C,
92R
Michael L. Smith 59TC
Dan Sudia 78C, 82C, 91L
Mary M. Thacher 38BR
Helen Williams 50TR
Bill Wilson 15

Tom Stack and Associates
Larry Ditto 30BR
John Gerlach 83R
G.C. Kelley 84L, 85BL
Anthony Mercieca 72L
A. Nelson 34BL, 67R, 68L, 69TR
Rod Planck 3CR, 11T, 56, 69BR, 71L,
78L
Milton Rand 89L, 92L
Leonard Lee Rue III 73L, 73R, 80C
John Shaw 14TL, 38TR
Charles G. Summers, Jr. 73C
Don and Pat Valenti 83L

CONTENTS

THE BIRDS AROUND US

The fascinating hobby of attracting birds can be as simple or as involving as you choose, from scattering birdseed on the ground to constructing feeding platforms and birdhouses to attract specific kinds of birds.

Every year millions of Americans discover the pleasures of attracting birds. In fact, according to a recent survey by the United States Department of the Interior, the appreciation of birds ranks second only to gardening as America's favorite pastime. What accounts for such an increase in the popularity of bird attracting as a hobby?

○ Birds add color, liveliness, and music to our gardens in all seasons.

○ Birds are wild creatures, and they bring an element of nature right into the yard, up close, where we can observe it every day.

○ Birds are fascinating. Children can acquire an early interest in nature by watching them flock to the backyard feeder, and even the seasoned naturalist can learn new things every day by observing birds around the home.

○ Birds are beneficial. They eat huge quantities of insects, and are one of the best natural means of keeping these pests under control.

○ Birds are easy to attract. A small investment of time and money will draw these fascinating creatures all year round.

About This Book

Understanding how birds survive in the wild, including what kinds of places they prefer to dwell in, increases our ability to attract them to the home. Chapter Two, "Birds in the Wild," is a primer on the specialized equipment with which birds make their way in the wild, and how they have adapted to their natural habitats.

Food, water, protective cover, and a sheltered place to raise their young are the basic requirements for any creature's survival. To attract birds, we need to provide them with the means to satisfy these needs around the garden. For most birds, plants are an essential element in determining where they spend their time. The selection of plants and their arrangement in the landscape are important in making a bird feel at home. Chapter Three, "Birds in the Garden," discusses some easy ways we can translate to our gardens what we have learned about a bird's preferred habitat in the wild. This chapter includes an extensive chart that shows what trees, shrubs, and vines are most attractive to our common garden birds.

The question of which birds prefer which foods has often been answered with confusion and misconceptions. The research of Dr. A. D. Geis, of the United States Fish and Wildlife Service, provides authoritative information on the seed preferences of wild birds. This research forms the basis of the discussion in Chapter Four, "Providing Food," of the relative desirability of types of birdseed. Also included is an extensive chart that shows at a glance which common garden birds prefer which seeds. The presentation of food can be almost as important as the kind of food you offer, and this chapter also gives pointers on which kind of bird feeder to use for the birds you most want to attract.

A reliable source of clean water is an essential ingredient in any bird-attracting program. In fact,

Left: A flock of finches rests in a tree during a snowstorm. Many birds are more sociable in the harsh days of winter, finding survival value in traveling in numbers.

As this Rose-breasted Grosbeak shows, attracting birds can be as easy as placing a few sunflower seeds on a stump.

water may attract more kinds of birds than any of the special foods we provide. Not all birds eat seeds or suet, but they all need to drink water. Chapter Five, "Providing Water," discusses the variety of ways in which you can supply this vital resource and add to the beauty of your garden at the same time.

Few aspects of bird behavior are as fascinating to us as courtship, nest building, and raising the young. Chapter Six, "Providing Nesting Sites," gives suggestions for making your garden more attractive to nesting birds, as well as information on buying, building, and placing birdhouses.

The "Gallery of Birds" presents specific, helpful information on 75 birds that are most likely to be attracted to the garden. Illustrated with a color photograph and a map showing where the bird may be found, each entry gives details on the habitat and the food, water, and nesting preferences of that bird.

Supplies for Attracting Birds

Attracting birds can be remarkably easy; with a feeder or two stocked with their favorite foods, and a birdbath for drinking and bathing, you are virtually assured of persuading some to come close to the house. But bird attracting offers many different levels of enjoyment and challenge. Attracting the widest possible variety of birds, or selectively attracting your favorites, and persuading them to live and nest in your garden, can be a source of unending discovery and adventure.

In response to the growing popularity of this hobby, a huge variety of equipment and supplies is available from bird clubs, garden supply and home improvement centers, by mail order, and even at many supermarkets. Bird feeders come in all styles, from simple platforms and suet cages to elaborate glassed-in feeders that attach to the window. High-quality foods, from seed mixtures to convenient, long-lasting suet-seed cakes, have been extensively tested for their attractiveness to birds. Birdbaths can be purchased from a huge array, from hanging dishes for balcony or window to tiers of waterfalls and easy-to-install plastic garden pools. Ready-made nesting boxes that really work are widely available for specific birds, from simple, rustic bluebird houses to complex "apart-

ment houses" for Purple Martins. A host of related supplies help us to deal with any problems that might come up, from special squirrel guards to netting designed for protecting garden fruits and vegetables from over-zealous customers. In fact, the monumental variety of bird-attracting supplies can be confusing; throughout this book, we offer tips on purchases, in addition to ideas for building your own.

More Equipment You May Need

As you become more and more involved in attracting and observing birds, you might find that you need some additional equipment. A pair of binoculars kept handy at your favorite viewing window will bring those shy visitors that hang around the fringes of your garden up close for better observation.

A field guide is essential to positive identification of a species, and many excellent ones are available. A good field guide should be pocket size and lightweight, strongly bound to withstand frequent use, with a stain- and water-resistant cover. Illustrations should be in full color and show distinguishing traits. Clear, concise descriptions are necessary for identifying a bird in its various forms, including

Bouts of bad weather in winter are especially stressful to birds, which must maintain a constant body temperature of about 105°F. This American Robin is increasing the efficiency of its feather insulation by fluffing its plumage.

Water is one of the best ways of attracting the widest variety of birds. Many, like this American Robin, seldom use the foods we can provide at the feeder, but are frequent guests at the birdbath.

male in breeding and nonbreeding plumage, female, juvenile, and geographical variations. The guide should be organized by bird families, not by habitats or plumage coloration. Before you buy a field guide, read the introduction to be sure that it uses the most recent authority for nomenclature, the American Ornithologists' Union Check-list of North American Birds, revised in July of 1982. Older books use the previous revision of 1957, which is considerably different and obsolete.

Keeping Track of Your Visitors

Well-kept records can greatly increase your enjoyment of your bird-attracting program. Records reveal what you are doing right and should continue, as well as unsuccessful approaches that are unnecessary or wasteful. Keeping notes also focuses your attention and gives your observations structure. If you want to get really involved, your notes can even provide valuable information welcomed by bird research organizations.

With a notebook, pen, binoculars, and field guide next to your favorite viewing window, you're all set. Each time you make an observation note the date, the time of day, and what the weather is like. Stagger your observation periods at different times of day to compile complete information on the schedules of birds. If you record the following information, you will soon have a fascinating profile of your garden visitors.

o Your feeding schedule, including date, time of day, quantity, and kind of feeder used for each type of food offered. Include brand names where applicable.

o Testing tray records. (See the discussion of testing trays on page 40.)

o Species notes, including where the birds are observed in the garden; what kind (or kinds) of feeders they prefer; the number of individuals observed; whether more than one species is present, and how the species interact; and any unusual behavior.

o Nesting records, including date first seen in the garden, location and type of nest, nesting materials used, date nest completed, number of eggs laid and when (if observable), number of young raised to maturity, and when they left the nest.

The study of birds is rich and fascinating, constantly providing new understanding about the natural world. Few fields welcome the many important contributions of "amateurs" as much as ornithology does.

BIRDS IN THE WILD

Birds are specialized creatures, with special needs. How they meet those needs in nature shows us how to offer food, water, and shelter in the garden.

Where in the natural world do the birds around our homes come from? What do they need, and how do they get it when they're not at the back yard feeder? Answering these questions better equips us to know just what things attract birds and how we can best provide those things around the home.

Like all creatures, birds require four basic things to survive: food, water, protection from the elements and danger, and a place to raise their young safely. In nature, birds go about fulfilling these needs in a perplexing variety of ways.

Birds have been around a long, long time—at least 140 million years. Over the eons of evolution they have acquired some traits and lost others to become enormously varied. About 8,650 species of birds have been identified in the world today, of which 796 live in North America. Even in the much smaller group of birds that frequent our gardens we are confronted with a mind-boggling variety of birds of all shapes, sizes, colors, and habits.

How Birds Meet Their Needs

Specialization in birds is a very complex subject, and there are many things that scientists still don't understand. Just looking at birds, however, and observing their behavior, can teach us much about attracting them. Inherited physical equipment and behavioral patterns, slowly shaped by the millenia of evolution, strongly affect what resources a bird can use to survive, and how and where it does so.

Food

Birds choose their menu from the wide variety of resources that nature provides. Foods they eat include insects, spiders, grubs and worms, nuts and seeds, soft fruits and berries, tree sap, flower nectar, the tender young leaves and buds of grass, trees, and shrubs, eggs and nestlings stolen from another bird's nest, other birds, fish, and small animals, and the corpses of small and large animals killed in other ways.

The bill of a bird is a clue to its food preference. The Northern Cardinal is an example of a group of birds commonly called *seedeaters*. These birds all have a strong, cone-shaped bill with an angled cutting edge at the base, well adapted for cracking hard, dry seeds. Other seedeaters with similar bills include the finches, grosbeaks, tow-

Left: With its sleek, slim body, long pointed wings, and wide-gaping mouth, the Barn Swallow is specialized for the aerial life. Feeding, drinking and even bathing on the wing, swallows spend more time in the air than any other songbird, and may fly as much as six hundred miles a day in search of food. Right: The Scarlet Tanager is a shy forest bird that spends most of its time high in deciduous trees, where it feeds on soft fruits and insects, occasionally descending to sheltered spots to drink and bathe.

hees, American sparrows, Indigo Bunting, Dark-eyed Junco, and Pine Siskin. These birds depend on seeds the year round, although they also eat insects, particularly in the spring and early summer when seeds are more scarce, and when developing young need the more concentrated protein that insects provide.

Woodpeckers have strong, sharp, chisel-like bills that are useful for probing and chipping into wood. With its bill the woodpecker can also detect delicate vibrations on any surface it touches, making it a perfect tool for both sensing and extracting wood-boring insects.

Brown Creepers have slender, down-curved, sharply pointed bills for probing into the crevices of tree bark for insects and their larvae. Swallows scoop insects out of the air with wide-gaping bills surrounded by bristles. The bills of American Robins and thrushes are poorly adapted for cracking hard seeds and nuts, so they eat mostly insects and soft fruits and berries. American Kestrels have sharp, curved beaks useful for tearing the flesh of the animals they eat. (The bill of a bird of prey is also called a *beak.*) Some birds, like American Crows, have generalized bills and can eat practically anything.

Of course, the shape of its bill isn't the only physical factor that determines a bird's choice of food. Strong fliers like swifts and swallows, which feed on the wing, eat almost nothing but flying insects. The owl's hearing is so acute that it can detect the location of a mouse under leaves in total darkness, and the direction of its movement as well. The American Robin can actually see the subtle movements of earthworms just below the surface of the soil. Much is still to be discovered about the sensory abilities of birds, and how they affect the food preferences of different species.

Water

All birds need to consume water to survive. A few desert birds not ordinarily found in gardens are able to extract all the water they need from hard, dry seeds, but most birds require frequent trips to a source of open water to drink.

In nature birds find their water in rivers, ponds, lakes, and streams, as well as in the more ephemeral sources of raindrops, puddles, dewdrops, snow, and in some

Cardinal

Brown Creeper

American Crow

Red-bellied Woodpecker

Purple Martin

American Kestrel

The shape of a bird's bill is a clue to the type of food it eats.

cases plant sap, nectar, and moist fruits. In the garden, the birdbath or pool may attract a greater variety of birds than any food we can provide.

Birds vary a great deal in the way they approach water. Some strong fliers, like swifts and swallows, dip into water while on the wing. Open expanses that allow unrestricted flight are most attractive to them. Others, particularly those species that dwell in dense woods and thickets, like the Wood Thrush and Brown Towhee, approach their water slowly, in a long, cautious process; they prefer water right next to cover. Most garden birds like a water source somewhere between the two extremes, far enough from surrounding vegetation to offer surveillance against a surprise attack, yet close enough for refuge. These birds often approach water by perching in a nearby tree, then dropping down for a quick drink and a splash, followed by preening.

Protective Cover

Sooner or later even the most dedicated flyer has to come back to earth, if only to breed. Because birds are so dependent on flight for safety, they are most vulnerable when they are "grounded" to rest, feed, or nest.

To a bird, protection means staying both comfortable and safe. We usually think of a bird's protection as intimately connected with the kind of plants that it seeks for cover. A Scarlet Tanager might find protection from the hot sun, or cold wind and rain, or the prying eyes of predators, high in the branches of a tree. A Bobwhite might take cover on the ground under a clump of grass. But protection can take many forms besides the cover of plants. Some birds hide and rest in geological formations, such as a cave used by Barn Swallows or a high rocky ledge that provides a refuge for Rock Doves.

Plumage is a bird's first defense against an often hostile environment. The dense covering of feathers that all birds have insulates them from the damp and cold, retains vital body heat, camouflages them from predators, and makes possible efficient flight.

Some birds, like the male Northern Cardinal and Northern Oriole, have colorful plumage all year round. The color of a bird's plumage, however, most often re-

Plumage color can be an important clue to the preferred cover of a bird species. The reddish brown upper body and tawny streaked breast of the Brown Thrasher blend well with the dry leaf litter and grasses of the shrubby undergrowth and brushpiles it frequents.

flects the kind of plant cover a bird seeks for protection. The greenish yellow of many warblers is difficult to distinguish from the sun-dappled foliage of the trees they inhabit. The dusky browns of thrushes and sparrows blend well with the piles of leaves and grasses they frequent under shrubs and thickets close to the ground.

The fact that females of nearly all bird species have developed plumage that blends with their environment shows that camouflage and inconspicuous plumage are a distinct advantage to birds. Many male birds, such as the Yellow Warbler and the American Goldfinch, exchange their bright breeding colors for duller ones in winter.

The kind of protective cover a bird uses is dictated by a host of factors besides plumage color, however. For example, the type of feet a bird has limits the surfaces it can move and rest on, and hence its choice of cover. Songbirds, which include about three-fifth of the world's known species, and many of our garden birds, are referred to by scientists as *perching birds*. This is a more accurate term, as some "songbirds" don't really sing, but they all have a specialized foot structure in which three toes point forward, and one toe points backward to oppose them. This foot structure makes them adept at clinging to cylindri-

cal objects like a tree twig or branch, or a grass stem. Nuthatches are perching birds with an even more specialized foot, with long toes and sharp claws that help make them expert climbers, even to the point of being able to climb down a tree trunk head first.

Quail are related to chickens, and have similar strong legs and long, clawed toes they use for scratching food from the ground. Although fast flyers for short distances, they are such good runners, walkers, and specialized ground-feeders that they apparently take to the air only when they have to. California Quail have been clocked running at twelve miles per hour. It is no accident that their preferred cover

The White-breasted Nuthatch is a perching bird whose specialized feet enable it to cling to the rough vertical surface of tree trunks, where these birds spend most of their time. Nuthatches are such adept clingers that they can climb down trunks headfirst, catching many tiny insects missed by other clinging birds.

is close to the ground in grasses and shrubs.

Chimney Swifts have feet with all four clawed toes pointing forward, enabling them to cling to rough, vertical surfaces like the inside of the hollow trees and chimneys in which they roost and nest. But the structure of their feet makes them virtually helpless on the ground. Most woodpeckers have four long toes, two pointing forward, two pointing backward for bracing, which they use for clinging and climbing on rough surfaces like tree trunks.

A Place to Raise the Young

No other bird activity fascinates bird lovers everywhere as much as building nests and raising young. The artistry and resourcefulness many birds display in nest building is among their most interesting characteristics, and the variety of techniques and materials used, and nesting sites chosen, is almost unbelievable. Types of nests range from the Rock Dove's rough platform of sticks and twigs on a high ledge to the elaborate cup nests of many songbirds, hidden in the crotch of a tree or shrub.

The lucky person who discovers a hummingbird nest realizes how the phrase "work of art" applies in the world of birds. Meticulously constructed of plant down and fine fibers, and decorated with moss and lichen, this minuscule nest is nearly impossible to distinguish from another bump on a limb. Enormous quantities of materials go into such a bit of a nest; one observer estimated some fifteen thousand miles of spider thread were used in one nest alone. We might think that such a feat would take a long time to accomplish, but one busy hummingbird was observed to build a nest in just three hours!

Woodpeckers dig out nesting holes in tree trunks, usually dead or dying ones, with their strong, sharp bills. Bluebirds, House Wrens, Black-capped Chickadees, and in fact, all the birds we build birdhouses for depend on the cavities made by woodpeckers, and other natural holes, to nest in. Modern practices of clean forestry, agriculture, and gardening in some areas have seriously reduced the number of dead or dying trees available to these birds.

Some birds, like Cliff Swallows and

Left: *In the wild, Barn Swallows build their mud nests on the steep, rocky walls of bluffs, cliffs, and caves, usually under an overhang and supported by a shallow ledge. Below: A dead willow snag provides a Redheaded Woodpecker with a place to raise its young.*

phoebes, attach their nests with sticky mud to vertical surfaces like cliff faces or banks cut by a river or stream. For these birds the availability of mud is a necessity. Birds that build cup nests in a tree or shrub may also require mud for construction. The female American Robin typically finishes off her handiwork with many trips to a source of mud, smearing it around and around the inside of the nest with her breast.

Orioles weave pendulous nests, suspended from the delicate tips of branches that seem scarcely able to support their weight. These sacklike structures are cunningly wrought from plant fibers and hair, tightly woven, and lined with plant down and soft feathers.

Perhaps the most familiar kind of bird nest is the cup nest tightly interwoven within the crotch of tree limbs or shrub branches. Some, like the nests of warblers and vireos, display amazing sophistication in tight, strong weaving patterns and choice of materials. The nest of the American Goldfinch is so tightly woven that it will hold water. In fact, if the parents are unable to return to the nest in time to protect the nestlings from rain, the young ones may drown.

Birds that build cup nests usually start with an underlying structure of sticks and twigs, to which they add an astounding array of building materials: grass, leaves, plant down (thistle down is a favorite of goldfinches), strips of bark, webs of spiders and tent caterpillars, pine needles, mosses, feathers, animal hair. Some birds, like titmice and orioles, will line their nests almost entirely with animal hair if given the chance; horse and cattle hair are favorites, and may be collected from living animals. Pets as well as wild and domestic animals are common subjects of "hair raids," and Tufted Titmice have been known to pull hair from human heads. When natural materials are scarce, birds can be quite resourceful with man-made stuff. String, yarn, tissue, and strips of cellophane are favorites. The availability of nesting materials can be an important criterion for choosing a nesting site.

Convenient sources of food and water are also vital factors in choosing where to raise a brood. Infant birds are exceedingly hungry for their size, eating as much as one and a half times their weight each day. Feeding them means many energy-draining trips for parents, so their food demands are also higher than usual. As with many seed-eaters that feed insects to their young, the dietary demands of young birds may be different from those of their parents—another important factor in the selection of a nest site.

Dry foods fed to infants are usually moistened first by the parent, so water demands as well are often greater at nesting time. Some parents even carry water to young in their beaks—a difficult task

Above left: This Northern Oriole has chosen an apple tree for its home. Wise gardeners and farmers welcome this bird; its prodigious consumption of insects is well worth the few fruits it eats. Above: The American Goldfinch depends on ripening thistle seeds for down to construct its nest, as well as for food to feed its young.

over any distance. It's no wonder that many garden birds prefer to nest near a source of drinking water.

From the time the egg is laid until the young bird is able to fend for itself is the most dangerous period of its life. Cold wind and rain are especially hazardous. Predation of eggs and young by other birds and animals takes a heavy toll too.

Birds choose nest sites that are protected from the elements and inaccessible to predators. Sometimes the nest site changes with the season. American Robins typically choose an evergreen for their first brood, for protection from the cold winds and rain of early spring. Later broods are usually raised in a deciduous tree, whose summer foliage offers greater protection from the sun. A high cliff, a dense, thorny shrub, and the end of a flimsy branch are examples of sites chosen for protection from predators. Nests are generally built in the same kind of cover that adults use the rest of the year for protection.

The connection between *how* a bird survives and its habitat, or *where* it does so, is intricate and complex. A bird's specialized behavior and physique may narrow and focus the resources it is able to use—for example, to exploit a plentiful food source that no other bird can use as efficiently. Availability of food, water, and protective cover are obviously important criteria for where a bird lives, but that availability depends on two things: its actual presence, and whether or not a bird is able to use it. Our goal is to persuade birds to live around our homes. If we understand where and under what conditions a bird chooses to live in the wild we are better equipped to attract that bird.

Above left: A Yellow Warbler has chosen an American hazel in which to construct its tightly woven cup nest. Above: These young Yellow Warblers still have traces of down feathers, which is not surprising considering that they leave the nest when they are only nine to twelve days old.

Swallows are among the earliest North American birds to gather for migration in the fall, as these Barn Swallows are doing in North Dakota. Some Barn Swallows have the longest migration route of any North American land bird, from Alaska to southern Argentina for a round-trip distance of 14,000 miles.

Range

The broad geographical area within which all the individuals of a species of bird are found is the *range* of that species. Years of observation by thousands of people across the country have been accumulated into *range maps* for each bird species found in North America. A range map is given for each bird described in the "Gallery of Birds," beginning on page 65. The boundaries of a range can be the result of many factors. Birds' movements are limited by physical obstacles, like mountain ranges or great bodies of water over which they cannot or will not fly. Climate too plays an important role in determining range. For example, the aridity of a desert climate might prove inhospitable to a particular species, while another might not be able to withstand cold conditions.

A bird's environment is seldom static; ranges can shift, dwindle, or grow under the influence of broad environmental changes, such as long-term climatic shifts or human alteration of the landscape. Ranges can also change seasonally. On one hand, the needs of a bird frequently change with the season; the specialized needs of nesting and breeding are often quite different from the more generalized needs of simply surviving. On the other hand, the habitat itself undergoes dramatic changes in available food, water, and plant cover as the seasons progress. Thus a species of bird can have more than one range, depending on the season. These ranges are usually called the *breeding range* and the *wintering range*, although these terms are a bit misleading. Some birds move into their wintering range soon after breeding is over, in late summer. Most birds stay around their breeding range for some time

after the young have left the nest. The area where the breeding and wintering ranges coincide, and where a species of bird may be seen the year round, is known as its *permanent range*.

Some birds, such as the Northern Cardinal, are *permanent residents* in a fairly restricted area, where individuals spend their entire lives, both summer and winter. Other species roam about from one place to another as conditions such as climate, food and water, and competition change locally. Only when the movement of a bird is regular and seasonal, however, is it called *migration*. The distance of migration may be short and local, as with the twice-annual hike of some quail up and down a mountainside. Or it may be dramatically long, like the yearly flight to South America of some swallows. Migration is an interesting specialization developed over thousands of years.

When migratory birds are occupying their summer, or breeding, range, they are called *summer residents*; when in their winter range they are called *winter residents*. When they are traveling in between, in an area not their summer or winter range, they are called *transients*.

Habitat

Knowing the range of a bird is just a start to understanding its habitat. The broad area on a map that indicates a bird's range is only a generality, with some concentrations of high populations, and other areas in which that bird may not be found at all. A bird's *habitat* is simply where it lives, including all the elements of its environment—plants, air, water, soil, climate, other birds, and animals. All of these elements interact in complex ways to form the unique habitat of a bird species.

Plants are a most important habitat element. They are a source of food for many birds, yielding fruits, berries, nuts, seeds, greens, sap, and nectar. Living plants and their decomposing remains are the main food of most insects, which in turn compose a large part of the diet of some birds. Plants provide nesting sites and comfortable resting spots, protecting birds from unfavorable climate and helping conserve their energy. They also provide a refuge from predators so that birds may venture forth to eat and drink. In some cases they even provide moisture in sap or nectar, or by collecting water from rain or dew.

Even during the breeding season the Pine Siskin is a gregarious bird, nesting in loose colonies in the coniferous forests of the mountains and far north. In winter they become even more social, and far less specific in choice of habitat. Flocks of 50 to 200 are common, and may number in the thousands.

Where Birds Live

Ecologists classify habitats in many different ways, from very broad categories such as forest or desert to very narrow subdivisions of enormous variety like the edge of a forest pool, or a desert oasis. In this chapter we discuss bird habitats for two purposes: to learn where those birds frequently found around our homes live in nature, and to relate those natural habitats to the combinations of plants and structures usually found in our gardens. Therefore we have excluded many habitats that are not really useful for attracting garden birds, like tundra or saltwater marshes. The following discussion focuses on two broad categories that have many different variations throughout the country: forest and open country.

As we have seen, birds tend to be specialized in where they live. Because they are such mobile creatures, however, few of our garden birds depend on a single resource or location to survive. Some of them make use of different resources in different seasons. Some birds find an advantage in exploiting a variety of resources. For example, a meadow might be rich in grass seeds and insects for food, while a nearby woodland might provide a nesting site.

The *edge* between two types of vegetation is the place where the advantages of both are most convenient. As we might expect, these areas tend to support the widest variety of bird species, as well as the greatest number of individuals.

Edges often occur gradually over distance. A woodland might blend into a grassland with gradually wider-spaced trees and shrubs over many miles. Or edges can occur abruptly, as with an isolated grove of trees in open country, or thickets adjoining a forest stream.

Abrupt edges can provide certain structural advantages to birds, such as a high spot to watch for danger or prey, or corridors for flight pathways. They may also supply islands of concentrated resources not as available in the region as a whole. The attractiveness of edges to birds is the chief reason we find so many of them in gardens, taking advantage of the rich variety of trees, shrubs, flower beds, hedges, lawns, and even buildings. In the discussion that follows, we have subdivided the two major natural habitats of garden birds into some edges they especially favor.

Birds of the Forest

A bird may inhabit a forest because of the kind of trees it finds there. Some of our garden birds, such as Pine Siskins and Purple Finches, prefer coniferous forests like the spruce, fir, and pine forests of high altitudes and the North. The western hemlock and redwood forests of the moist Pacific Coast are home to birds like the Varied Thrush. Other species of birds, such as Blue Jays and Red-eyed Vireos, are found

The Steller's Jay is a bird of deep forests in the western United States. Like its eastern relative, the Blue Jay, this member of the Crow family is an important sentinel to the forest community, quick to warn of danger.

mostly in deciduous forests, like the beech-maple forests of the Northeast or the drier oak-hickory forests of the Midwest. Many of our garden birds that live in dense forests, however, prefer mixed forests of both evergreen and deciduous trees. Evening Grosbeaks, for example, depend on the seeds of both maples and conifers.

A forest, moreover, includes other kinds of plants besides trees. Under the canopy of trees grow a number of layers of understory plants, including smaller shade-tolerant trees and shrubs, and ground-covering plants adapted to even less light, scattered throughout the thick leaf litter of the forest floor. Birds often favor a particular forest layer. Scarlet Tanagers, for example, spend most of their time in high treetops. Wood Thrushes, whose large eyes are well adapted to the gloom, forage under shrubs on the forest floor.

Extent is another quality that defines a forest for many birds. Some shy forest dwellers rarely seen around gardens require many square miles of uninterrupted forest. Most of the garden birds that dwell in forests, however, readily cross spaces between broken forest and scattered trees to inhabit smaller woodlands, or take to more open areas in winter. Those birds listed on our chart as deep-forest dwellers are most likely to be found in gardens with trees that are close to a more extensive woodland.

Forest Openings: Forest openings and margins, such as a space where trees have been logged, or a grassy meadow, or a pocket of bedrock or sandy, poor soil that doesn't support the demands of trees, are important edge formations in the forest. For many birds these edges provide expanded and varied resources. Black-capped Chickadees feed on the seeds of sun-loving grasses as well as on pine seeds. American Robins forage for earthworms in the moist soils of meadows and woodland glens, while nesting in trees at the edge. Screech Owls tend to hunt over open spaces, while nesting and roosting in trees.

Forest openings are generally characterized by both density and variety of shrubs, small trees, and herbaceous plants that thrive in sunlight. Especially at the margins of these openings, where the shade-tolerant plants of the deep forest grow more vigorously in greater light and

merge with the sun-loving plants out in the open, the vegetation is most dense and varied. Such areas offer expanded resources for birds in the form of a greater variety of fruits and seeds; more insects that feed on the plants; and a wider choice of nesting sites and cover. Where dense forests border open country, we usually find populations of birds from both habitats.

Openings, especially those with low-growing vegetation, increase visibility for forest-dwelling birds. This can work two ways: increased danger because birds are

*Top: **Dense undergrowth is important to many birds of lower forest strata, like this Hermit Thrush nesting on the forest floor.** Above: **A Rufous-sided Towhee is approaching a small spring for a drink.***

Above: *Open fields of herbaceous plants and brush are rich in food for birds. This American Goldfinch is dining on the seeds of a sunflower.* Above right: *Blackberries are one of the first "pioneer" shrubs to invade old fields, and are a favorite plant of many birds. The Gray Catbird, for example, commonly nests in them, and relishes the fruit.*

more readily spotted, especially by airborne predators like the American Kestrel; and increased safety through better detection of predators, especially ground-moving hunters. The result is to encourage more time spent at the margins of openings; many forest dwellers make only quick forays out into the open.

Open spaces lend themselves well to this dash-and-hide movement, as flight is less restricted than in dense forest. Whether openings are long and linear, like a roadway or utility right-of-way, or closed and circular, birds often use them as flight pathways and corridors to make their way through a broken forest, racing through the more exposed open spaces to the greater protection of woodland on the other side.

Forest Watersides: A special group of forest-opening habitats are those created by bodies of water, such as lakes, ponds, rivers, or streams. Not only does water provide opportunities for drinking and bathing, and foster more insect life for food, but the moister soil around its edge encourages a greater abundance and variety of plants. Unrestricted flight space and better surveillance of ground-moving predators are qualities of openings in general that are enhanced by water.

The bottomland woods bordering a river or wide stream are especially inviting to certain birds. Trees common to the bottomland woods of the East include sycamores, elms, ashes, tupelo, and maples. These trees, which are quite tolerant of water-logged, compacted soils, are commonly planted to line our suburban streets. The Northern Oriole prefers to nest in American elms, the Screech Owl in sycamores.

Birds of Open Country

A few garden birds almost never leave the cover of brush, and live in thick, uninterrupted areas of shrubbery. The Wrentit, a common garden bird in the West, is rarely seen outside the cover of a shrub, and seldom crosses open spaces of more than a few feet. And a few birds sometimes found in gardens, like swifts and swallows, which hunt on the wing, prefer open grasslands without obstructions to their flight. But most birds of open country that we see about the garden (see the chart on page 20) prefer mixed brushlands, in which patches of shrubs and small trees are interrupted with patches of grass and wildflowers.

As with forest, shrubby open-country habitats vary tremendously in the kinds of plants they support, and hence in the variety of birds likely to be found there. Abandoned agricultural fields in the East, with a mix of grasses, wildflowers, shrubs, and small trees, provide a tremendous variety of heights at which birds can forage and hide, as well as a profusion of rich food-bearing plants. Junipers, hawthorns, wild blackberries, and blueberries provide fruits for birds like the Bobwhite, Northern Mockingbird, and Cedar Waxwing. Wildflowers such as sunflowers, asters, and goldenrod provide seeds in fall and winter for birds like the American Goldfinch and Indigo Bunting.

The dense evergreen shrubs dominated by scrub oaks and manzanita of the Pacific coastal chaparral, the sagebrush of the western plains, and the mesquite and cactus scrub of the desert Southwest are examples of habitats dominated by shrubs and grasses—in part because of scarce water to support more demanding trees. A wide variety of birds make their homes in these areas. Some, like the California Quail, Cactus Wren, Bushtit, Wrentit, and Brown Towhee, are found only in these western habitats. Others, like the White-crowned Sparrow, Northern Mockingbird, and House Finch, are also found in the moister brushlands of the North and the East. Where the ranges of two similar birds overlap, they often live in different parts of a habitat. For example, the Rufous-sided Towhee shares its range with the Brown Towhee in parts of the Southwest. There it inhabits areas of tall shrubs, like scrub oaks, while the Brown Towhee resides in low ones.

In shrubby habitats the edge-counterpart to the opening of a forest is the island, or prominence, such as a grove of trees or even a single isolated tree. A utility pole or even a fencepost is a sort of prominence that might make very open country inhabitable to some birds, such as the Red-headed Woodpecker, which often nests in such places, or the Northern Mockingbird, which uses a perch for territorial song.

Many of the birds that frequent forest openings are also found in the islands of refuge provided by groves of trees in open country. Birds that roam about use such groves as stopping-off places. Other birds more comfortable in open areas use such islands for the additional food and cover they provide. Some, like the American Kestrel, require such groves for nesting.

Particularly in the drier shrubby habitats of the West, there is often a close connection between such "island" habitats and water. Water flows off the hard surface of a rock outcrop and concentrates at its periphery, sometimes in enough volume to support denser vegetation than the surrounding area, or even a grove of trees. Water may build up only seasonally, as with a desert wash, but still be stored beneath the soil surface, resulting in the dense vegetation that is characteristic of such places.

In open country, the vegetation encouraged by the year-round water of rivers and streams, and the springs and pools of oases, creates dense islands of resources for many birds. Although the list of birds that use such open-country formations is somewhat different from those that use forest waterside openings, the expansion of resources offered by the lush vegetation is quite similar, including increased protective cover, greater feeding opportunities, and protected flight corridors.

Many open-country garden birds seem to prefer waterside thickets, but frequently reside in similar habitats in which water is absent. Yellow Warblers and Song Sparrows, for example, can often be found in roadside and fencerow shrubbery, and in the hedges and shrub borders of our gardens.

In similar ways, many beautiful birds find expanded and more various ways to thrive around our homes and in our gardens, and that is the subject of the next chapter.

Many birds, like this American Kestrel surveying the first flurry of a snowstorm, depend on prominences in open country. Such a prominence can be as simple as a fencepost, utility pole, isolated tree, or housetop.

Birds That Visit the Garden and Their Preferred Natural Habitats

In this chart and the accompanying text bird habitats are categorized to provide information that we can use to attract birds to the home landscape. The text parallels the chart in breaking down the natural habitats and relating them to the plant groupings found in our gardens. The chart can also be used to predict which birds are most likely to be found in a particular kind of landscape.

As you will note, few of the species listed here exhibit a strong preference for only one kind of habitat. Even for those that do, it would be misleading to say that they can't be found elsewhere. The Wood Thrush, for example, strongly prefers moist woodlands with nearby water, such as a stream or pool, but it can also be found in drier woodlands, and even in relatively open country under dense shrubs.

Some birds use one kind of habitat for breeding, and another kind for winter foraging. The Yellow-rumped Warbler, for example, can be found in many kinds of open-country habitats in winter, but it retreats to dense mixed forest for breeding. Many birds, in fact, are most specific about habitat choice during the stressful time of breeding, and more willing to explore different places after the young have flown.

Other birds find similar resources in what, to our eyes, are quite different habitats. The edge of an isolated grove in open country, for instance, is frequently used in much the same way as the edge of a deep forest opening.

	OPEN COUNTRY				FOREST					
	Waterside Vegetation	Isolated Prominence, Grove Trees	Mixed Brush and Grass	Margin on Open Country	Waterside Vegetation	Broken; openings	Deep Mixed	Deep Coniferous	Deep Deciduous	
American Crow		●			●	●				
American Goldfinch		●	●	●		●				
American Kestrel		●		●						
American Robin		●		●		●				
American Tree Sparrow	●		●	●						
Anna's Hummingbird	●				●	●				
Barn Swallow	●									
Bell's Vireo	●		●	●						
Black-capped Chickadee		●				●	●			
Black Phoebe	●				●					
Blue Jay							●	●		
Brown Creeper							●	●	●	
Brown Thrasher			●	●						
Brown Towhee	●		●							
Bushtit	●		●	●						
Cactus Wren	●		●							
California Quail	●	●	●							
Carolina Chickadee		●				●	●			
Carolina Wren		●		●		●				
Cedar Waxwing	●	●	●	●		●				
Chestnut-backed Chickadee					●			●		
Chimney Swift	●									
Chipping Sparrow	●		●							
Cliff Swallow	●									
Common Grackle		●	●		●	●				
Dark-eyed Junco		●	●	●	●	●	●	●		
Downy Woodpecker					●	●	●			
Eastern Bluebird		●		●						
Eastern Phoebe					●					
European Starling		●	●							

	OPEN COUNTRY				FOREST				
	Waterside Vegetation	Isolated Prominence, Grove Trees	Mixed Brush and Grass	Margin on Open Country	Waterside Vegetation	Broken, openings	Deep Mixed	Deep Coniferous	Deep Deciduous
Evening Grosbeak							●		●
Golden-crowned Kinglet				●		●			●
Gray Catbird	●	●		●					
Hermit Thrush						●	●	●	●
House Finch		●	●						
House Sparrow		●	●						
House Wren				●	●	●			
Indigo Bunting	●		●	●		●			
Mourning Dove	●	●		●					
Northern Bobwhite		●	●	●					
Northern Cardinal	●	●	●	●					
Northern Flicker	●	●		●		●			
Northern Mockingbird		●		●					
Northern Oriole	●	●			●	●			
Orchard Oriole	●	●			●				
Pine Siskin		●		●		●		●	
Plain Titmouse		●		●			●		
Purple Finch	●	●			●	●	●		●
Purple Martin	●								
Red-bellied Woodpecker					●	●			
Red-breasted Nuthatch							●		●
Red-eyed Vireo		●		●		●		●	
Red-headed Woodpecker	●	●		●	●				
Red-winged Blackbird	●		●						
Rose-breasted Grosbeak		●		●	●	●			
Ruby-crowned Kinglet				●		●			●
Ruby-throated Hummingbird					●	●			
Rufous Hummingbird				●	●	●			
Rufous-sided Towhee	●		●	●		●			
Scarlet Tanager							●		
Screech Owl				●	●	●			
Scrub Jay		●	●						
Song Sparrow	●	●	●						
Steller's Jay								●	●
Summer Tanager					●	●			
Tree Swallow	●								
Tufted Titmouse		●			●		●	●	
Varied Thrush					●				●
Warbling Vireo	●	●							
Western Bluebird		●		●		●			
White-breasted Nuthatch							●	●	
White-crowned Sparrow	●		●						
White-eyed Vireo	●	●	●	●		●			
White-throated Sparrow	●		●			●			
Winter Wren					●				●
Wood Thrush					●				
Wrentit	●		●						
Yellow-bellied Sapsucker					●	●			
Yellow-rumped Warbler		●		●		●	●		
Yellow Warbler	●	●		●		●			

BIRDS IN THE GARDEN

Plants are the most important element in the garden—to birds as well as to you. No matter what size your garden is, whether it's formal or naturalistic in style, you can use plants to enhance its attractiveness to birds.

There's no doubt about it, a wide variety of birds love the home landscape. Chances are that your home grounds already suit the tastes of many species, since our human ideals of beauty and usefulness in the garden frequently result in concentrations of food, water, and shelter that are particularly appealing to birds.

Plants, of course, are the chief element of the garden and are also the number one priority of birds. It's likely that many of the plants you already have, both native and exotic, are quite attractive to birds. Most of the qualities that humans value in plants, such as abundant fruit and flower production, density of growth, and long-lasting foliage, are also qualities that birds find useful. As horticulturists intensify these qualities through breeding and selection of native plants, the garden resources of birds are improved. Because we also use many exotic plants—those native to distant regions—our gardens provide birds with an abundance and variety of food and shelter not found in their natural habitats. Even if all you have is a lone pyracantha bush, you are providing birds with an attractive fruit they could not find in the American wild.

The rich soil, water, and fertilizer that we lavish on our gardens promote a lushness of growth and abundance of food that birds seldom find in the natural world. Because our gardens are limited in space, and because we support them with extra care, food-producing plants are usually more densely concentrated in gardens than in nature.

The home landscape, with its combination of plants, open space, and buildings, offers many parallels to natural bird habitats. In their density, lush good health, and variety, the plants in our gardens often resemble the waterside growth so attractive to many birds, especially in combination with the open spaces of lawns and the vertical, clifflike surfaces of walls. In the western part of the country, where natural habitats consist largely of grassland, brush, and scrub, even a lone garden tree can be an important bird refuge. In that dry, sparse country, a garden with only a few plants can perform many of the same functions for birds as a natural oasis or grove. In the eastern part of North America, where natural habitats are dominated by dense forest, an open lawn can be an attractive feature for birds of forest edges and openings, which outnumber all other kinds of garden birds.

The surrounding countryside and the kinds of bird habitats it supports are important in determining the kinds of birds that you will be able to attract to your home grounds. After all, birds are not great respecters of fences and property lines. Because they tend to exploit a variety of resources, nearby areas—a neighbor's pond or grove of trees, a golf course, wildlife refuge, park, forest, or agricultural fields and pastures—will greatly influence the number and types of birds that can be enticed to your garden.

Just as birds don't notice our human boundaries, winging their way across the tallest fences, neither are they concerned with our human concepts of style and beauty. No matter what style of garden you have, from the rigidly formal to the

Left: The scarlet firethorn (Pyracantha coccinea) is an "exotic" landscape plant imported from the Mediterranean area and western Asia. Yet many birds, like this American Robin, immediately recognize its value as a food plant, and for thorny nesting protection.

wildly naturalistic, your garden functions in many of the ways that natural habitats do for birds.

Even though your garden may already be hospitable to many birds, by intensifying the resources that attract them you can encourage a wider variety of birds to spend more time there. Feeding stations, water, and birdhouses and nesting materials are discussed in the following chapters. This chapter discusses garden plants as a means of attracting birds—their selection, placement, variety, and relationship to one another.

Even if you have no intention of changing the plants in your yard, you will still find this chapter useful in evaluating why your garden attracts birds, and why they tend to congregate in certain places. Locating and intensifying these nodes of bird activity will help you make your garden more attractive to birds with minimal effort. No matter what style of garden you have, or what stage of development it is in, you can modify it through the selection and placement of plants.

The Elements of the Landscape

The ideal bird garden in the box on page 25 illustrates a typical home landscape that contains the elements common to many gardens throughout the country—trees, shrubs, flower beds, lawn, a house, and the paving of patio, drive, and walk. Perhaps the plants in your garden are not mature, or perhaps you are even starting out to establish a new landscape. Time has a way of solving that kind of problem, and even the youngest landscape can be quite attractive to birds. Your garden may be tiny compared to an average suburban lot; but

Top left: The shy Indigo Bunting occasionally emerges from shrubbery, tall grass, and flowers to visit nearby lawns, where it consumes large quantities of insects and weed seeds. Above: The Northern Bobwhite is another common bird on lawns, particularly when a habitat of open brushland and fields is available nearby. Top right: The American Robin is also a familiar sight on lawns, relentless in its search for earthworms.

even if all you have is a windowsill, deck, or urban courtyard, you can still "borrow" birds from neighbors and nearby habitats. In fact, no individual bird landscape, no matter how ideal, can be considered as anything but a part of a much larger "bird garden" that is at least neighborhood-sized. The surrounding neighborhood and countryside help to determine the character of the garden, both for continuity, to appeal to birds likely to be in the area, and for contrast, to give them something special that they may have difficulty finding nearby. In different regions of the country, the context of your garden will be entirely different. The point is that whatever you have to work with, you can maximize your home's bird-attracting potential.

Ideally, the bird landscape has three main qualities. First, it provides abundantly and in a variety of ways the resources that birds need—food, water, protection from the elements and danger, and a place to raise the young safely. Second, it concentrates these resources in locations that offer the best opportunities for bird watching, either close to the house and patio, or in areas where the observer can comfortably hide. Third, this garden includes a variety of vegetation types.

The discussion of garden elements is divided into three major sections: shady gardens composed mostly of trees, paralleling the discussion of forest habitats in the previous chapter; open gardens planted mostly with shrubs and lawn, paralleling the discussion of open country; and small gardens. Mixed gardens containing features of all three may be the most common of all. For specific suggestions on what plants are most attractive to birds, consult the chart on page 32, and the lists on page 30.

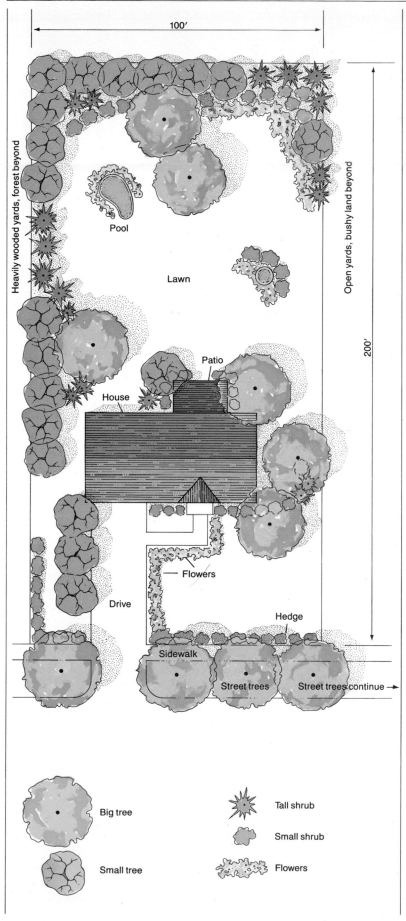

100'

Heavily wooded yards, forest beyond

Open yards, bushy land beyond

200'

Pool

Lawn

Patio

House

Flowers

Drive

Hedge

Sidewalk

Street trees

Street trees continue →

Big tree

Small tree

Tall shrub

Small shrub

Flowers

The Ideal Bird Garden

When it comes to bird gardening, no single "ideal" is applicable to all situations. This plan is presented, not because it might fit your location exactly, but to illustrate some important concepts about what birds find attractive. This ideal garden provides food, cover, and nesting sites in a variety of ways, and is richly stocked with the plants birds like the most (see the chart on page 32).

This garden capitalizes on the surrounding countryside. Off to the left are older homes with a lot of mature trees, and a forested park beyond. To the right are newer homes with shrubs and lawns, with some abandoned agricultural fields farther away that will eventually be developed into new homes. If it were completely surrounded by a forested neighborhood, this garden might be seen as a large "woodland opening." If it were completely surrounded by open lands, it might be seen as an isolated grove, or an oasis.

This garden capitalizes on the popularity with birds of edges. The garden itself lies at the transition between two major habitats, and a variety of edge formations are especially pronounced features. The "woodland opening" at the upper left is intensified by dense plantings of understory shrubs and small trees, and the addition of a small pool. The "oasis" in the back lawn, and the "riverside" of street trees and hedges at the front, are also excellent places to incorporate water. The house is surrounded with dense foundation shrubs and vines and a small grove of trees to resemble the "prominence" of lush plants around a rock outcrop. Where one type of vegetation merges into another, such as lawn into the "forest edge" at the upper right, is an excellent spot to concentrate resources like bird feeders. Ideally, these transitional zones should be within easy view of the house.

If Your Garden Is Mostly Trees

You have an advantage with your heavy stand of trees in attracting birds of the forest—a feature many homeowners wait a lifetime for. Nuthatches, Brown Creepers, thrushes, and tanagers are only a few of the special birds that may visit your woodland garden.

As we saw in Chapter 2, "Birds in the Wild," edges, openings, and understory layers are very appealing to many garden birds, and these transitional zones are an important feature of the garden. Where mature trees abut the open area of a lawn we often plant borders of shrubs and flowers, resembling the thickets of woodland margins. A pocket of lawn protruding into the shady part of the garden, so that it is partially ringed by trees, resembles a woodland opening. Other low, open areas, like the paving of patio and driveway, or plantings of ground covers or flower beds, bordered with trees and shrubs, also function as woodland openings.

Birds frequently use the smooth, flat surfaces of lawn or pavement in some of the same ways they use wet meadows or bodies of water. You can intensify the "waterside" aspects of these garden elements with especially lush plantings of hedges and shrub borders at their margins. Where these "watersides" are close to trees we are likely to find hummingbirds, phoebes, titmice, and orioles, to name only a few.

By intensifying the edge effect of forest openings, watersides, and understory layers we can make the woodland garden even more attractive to birds.

o Plant a few clusters of shade-loving small trees, shrubs, and ground covers under your taller trees to provide a number of layers for different kinds of birds. (See the lists on page 30.)

o Leave some of your "forest floor" in open soil, or mulched with leaf litter, to provide an important resource for ground-foraging forest dwellers like thrushes. This is good for your plants, too.

o Add a few trees to change the proportion of your woodland closer to half evergreen, half deciduous. You can also use the understory layer you are adding to even out the balance of evergreen and deciduous plants.

o Take advantage of the openings already built into your landscape by planting their margins with dense shrubs and hedges especially attractive to birds. Lawns, patios, the street, the drive, and walks are all candidates for this treatment. These are also excellent places to increase the effect of "waterside" habitats.

o If you are especially ambitious and have no real open spots in your garden, you might consider creating an opening by removing a few trees. If you do decide to remove a dead tree or even a living one to create an opening, consider leaving a 12- to 15-foot stump with a few 2-foot side branches left on it to house some birds that dwell in tree cavities. However, if the tree you removed suffered from root rot you'd better cut it clear to the ground, as the stump is likely to fall over soon.

If Your Garden Is Mostly Shrubs and Lawn

Sunny, open gardens, with areas of lawn broken up by shrubs, flowers, and small fruiting trees, are most likely to attract birds of neighboring open country, such as quail, Mockingbirds, American Goldfinches, and American Sparrows. In the previous chapter we saw that prominences like groves, oases, and even isolated trees, as well as patches of shrubs mixed with grassy areas, are important edges for open-country birds. In many open gardens these features are already an important part of the landscape.

A sunny, open expanse of lawn is often interrupted with an "oasis"—a cluster of shrubs and flowers. The house itself is a kind of "island," or prominence, and in many gardens its functional resemblance to a rock outcrop is increased by dense foundation plantings of trees, shrubs, and vines. Birds that might be drawn to our garden "islands" include the Red-headed Woodpecker, Northern Flicker, Black-capped Chickadee, and Warbling Vireo. Shrubby "waterside vegetation," like a hedge along a drive, may be frequented by Yellow Warblers, Northern Cardinals, Song Sparrows, and Carolina Wrens, among others.

Here are some things you can do to heighten the effects of your garden prominences, oases, groves, and watersides.

o Start by intensifying the prominence you already have—the house. This is an excellent place to start a "grove" by planting a few trees. Also plant foundation shrubs and vines if you don't already have them. (For a list of vines that attract birds, see page 31.)

o Be sure to leave spaces or "clearings" between foundation plants and view windows. These are excellent spots to concentrate bird resources and leave sightlines open to the yard beyond.

o Away from the house, but within viewing distance, establish a second "prominence" by planting an isolated, fast-growing tree, such as a honey locust, pin oak, or red maple. Even more effective, especially right away, would be to plant a small grove of five or seven young trees (odd numbers look best in a grouping). If you already have an isolated tree in your yard, it can be made even more attractive to birds, if you have the space, by ringing it with a few younger trees of the same kind, as if they were saplings in a developing grove. (For a list of fast-growing trees to plant in small groves, see page 31.)

o If your garden is densely planted with large, uninterrupted beds of shrubs, consider removing some and replacing them with a lawn and beds of flowers to simulate natural flight paths. Openings in brush and scrub habitats are as important to birds as those in woodlands; brushy habitats broken up by grassy patches are preferred by many more birds than are solid shrubs.

Below left: *Elderberries* (Sambucus *species) are favored by many birds, such as this Warbling Vireo. These plants are also attractive in the garden for their large white flower heads in mid-summer and their purplish or bright red fruit.* **Below:** *The Eastern Bluebird prefers the open country of old fields, where brushy areas and patches of grass are interrupted by an occasional small tree.*

- Vary the height, density, and fruiting season of your shrub beds by planting taller shrubs, small fruiting trees, and lower ground covers. (For a list of appropriate plants, see page 31.)
- At the garden gate, or in a quiet sitting area of the yard, a small arbor planted with vines can provide another attractive spot for birds. A nesting shelf for robins or song sparrows is particularly appropriate here.
- If your landscape is mostly lawn, planting a central island of shrubs and flowers and a small fruiting tree is a quick and easy way to make it more attractive to birds. A birdbath and feeder will intensify its usefulness.
- If you're especially ambitious, planting generous beds of shrubs and flowers will do much to increase your lawn's attractiveness to birds. Or you can plan now to establish your whole garden as a large woodland grove with a central clearing, and let birds enjoy its young effect as a shrubby habitat while you wait for it to mature.
- If you have hedges, this is one place where informality is preferred by birds. Leave them unclipped, or prune them naturally by selective branch removal. Restrict your pruning to winter, if possible, after any fruit they produce has been eaten, and birds are not nesting. Shrubs that form next year's flower buds soon after blooming, however, will need to be pruned immediately after they bloom. It is best to avoid this kind of shrub for bird-attracting hedges.
- If you have flower beds, leave as many of the spent flowers as possible to provide food for birds when the seeds ripen. Plant perennials and annuals favored by birds, especially those whose seed heads are an asset to the fall and winter garden, like ornamental grasses. (For a list of such plants, see page 30.)

If You Have a Small Garden

The small garden can be a haven in an urban neighborhood, a welcome pocket of life to birds in a habitat that most closely resembles barren rocky canyons. Even the spot of green in a windowbox can attract the attention of passing birds and keep them coming back if extra resources are provided. The variety of wildlife that braves the concrete of our cities is amazing. You're fortunate if you live near a park or greenbelt, but it's not necessary for attracting birds. They will seek you out if you supply food, water, protective cover, and sheltered nesting sites.

- It doesn't take much space to plant a small haven. A perimeter of small trees around a patch of lawn, with a tiny pool in one corner backed by an especially dense planting of shrubs, small trees, and flowers, is within the reach of many urban dwellers.
- If you have a deck or a terrace, planter boxes with flowers and both deciduous and evergreen shrubs can make it resemble a ledge on a cliff that has caught a bit of soil, seeds, and water. A small tree in a tub can increase the effect of your mini-oasis. The greenery you provide will attract birds' attention, but you will have to supply concentrated resources of food and water to keep them returning. Many birdbaths and feeders fit nicely on terraces and are attractive to humans as well. (For a list of dwarf and compact plants, see page 31.)
- If all you have is a windowsill, you can still attract birds. Flower boxes can provide a green spot to draw the attention of passing birds, and flowers for hummingbirds to feed on. Window bird feeders and hummingbird feeders, and a small pan of water about 12 inches in diameter, will keep them coming back for more.

Below left: **In this Washington, D.C. garden fountain grass and showy stonecrop are a beautiful winter asset, as well as food for birds.** *Below:* **If you can allow an out-of-the-way corner of your garden to go a little wild, you may attract a ground-nesting resident. This clutch of California Quail eggs may have been laid by several females, but will be raised by only one breeding pair.** *Bottom right:* **The Song Sparrow is likely to deliver its beautiful song nearly anywhere, at any time. It commonly nests in the shrubs, tall grass, and dense flower borders of open gardens.**

Protecting Your Crops

If you are serious about raising vegetables, fruits, and berries, you'll need to protect your crops. The fact is that birds love most of the same fruits we do, and teaching them to come to your garden is an open invitation to raid your orchard and berry patch.

There are some steps you can take to protect your crop from birds. Bird netting is the most practical and effective way to protect both trees and shrubs. These mesh nets can be purchased at most garden centers. Birds often eat the flowers of fruit and nut trees as well as those of shrubs, greatly reducing their yield, so put up the nets as soon as the flowers start to open. Throw the netting directly over the tree. To protect your rows of berry-producing shrubs and vines, build a frame of 2 × 2's around the plants and cover the frame with bird netting.

Grapes can be protected by enclosing each developing cluster in a paper or cheesecloth bag as soon as the fruit sets. Protect corn in the same way after the ears are pollinated. Don't use plastic bags; heat and moisture will build up inside them.

Other tactics, such as hanging shiny objects like pie plates to flap in the wind, or suspending lifelike rubber snakes, may work for a while. Or make a framework of stakes on both sides of a row of fruits or vegetables and tie string between them in a crisscross pattern. Birds are discouraged from flying in between the strings. To further discourage them, hang strips of aluminum foil from the strings.

Seed-eating birds such as sparrows find newly planted seeds a tasty snack. Protect your crop by placing plastic netting over the seed bed. The netting should be removed soon after the seeds sprout, before the plants get too big. For smaller seed beds, cages of wire mesh can be placed over freshly planted seed and left on until the plants develop several sets of mature leaves. Cages about 10 × 10 × 24 inches are self-supporting; larger ones need to be reinforced with heavy wire.

Not all birds are destructive in the garden. Many species feed primarily on insects; in fact, birds are one of nature's most effective ways of controlling these harmful pests.

Fruits, berries, and vegetables are as appealing to birds as they are to people. Here are some measures you can take to protect your crops.

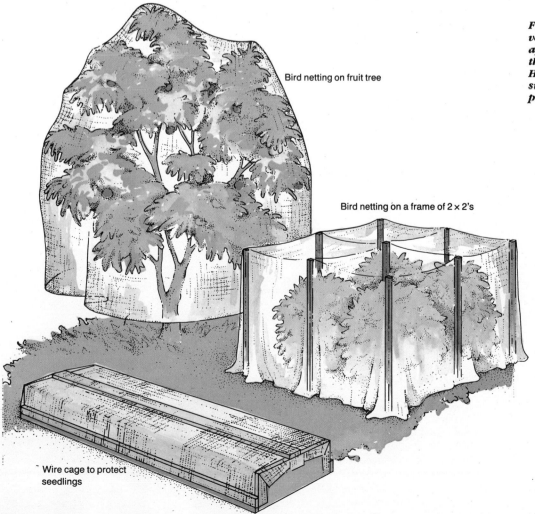

Bird netting on fruit tree

Bird netting on a frame of 2 × 2's

Wire cage to protect seedlings

Selected Plants for the Bird Garden

The plants on these lists have been chosen for their usefulness and attractiveness to birds and to gardeners alike. The Latin name is included in parentheses so you can look up the plant in garden books for further information on how to grow it. To find out which plants grow best in your area, and which varieties will best fill your specific needs, see Ortho's series of gardening books, available at your nursery or garden center.

Above: *Cedar Waxwing on scarlet firethorn* (Pyracantha). Top: Rudbeckia hirta *'Double Gold,' sometimes called "coneflower" for its beautiful winter seedheads.*

Annuals for Flowers and Seeds

(○ Especially beautiful in seed)

- ○ Amaranthus (*Amaranthus*, all species)
- Bachelor Button (*Centauria cyanus*)
- Calendula (*Calendula officinalis*)
- California Poppy (*Eschscholzia californica*)
- China Aster (*Callistephus chinensis*)
- Coreopsis (*Coreopsis*, all species)
- Cosmos (*Cosmos*, all species)
- ○ Gloriosa Daisy (*Rudbeckia hirta* var. *pulcherrima* 'Gloriosa Daisy')
- Grasses
  - ○ Quaking Grass (*Briza maxima*)
  - ○ Love Grass (*Eragrostis tef*)
  - ○ Hare's Tail Grass (*Lagurus ovatus*)
  - ○ Crimson Fountain Grass (*Pennisetum setaceum*)
  - ○ Plains Bristle Grass (*Setaria macrostachya*)
- ○ Love-in-a-mist (*Nigella damascena*)
- Marigold (*Tagetes*, all species)
- Pink (*Dianthus*, all species)
- Portulaca (*Portulaca grandiflora*)
- ○ Sea Lavender (*Limonium*, all species)
- ○ Sunflower (*Helianthus*, all species)
- Zinnia (*Zinnia*, all species)

Perennials for Flowers and Seeds

(○ Especially beautiful in seed)

- ○ Aster (*Aster*, all species)
- ○ Black-eyed Susan (*Rudbeckia*, all species)
- ○ Butterfly flower (*Asclepias tuberosa*)
- Chrysanthemum (*Chrysanthemum*, all species)
- Columbine (*Aquilegia*, all species)
- Coreopsis (*Coreopsis*, all species)
- ○ Goldenrod (*Solidago*, all species)
- ○ Globe Thistle (*Echinacea*, all species)

- Grasses
  - ○ Little Blue Stem (*Andropogon scoparius*)
  - ○ Bulbous Oatgrass (*Arrhenatherum elatius* var. *bulbosum*)
  - ○ Pampas Grass (*Cortedaria selloana*)
  - ○ Tufted Hair Grass (*Deschampsia caespitosa*)
  - ○ Eulalia Grass (*Miscanthus*, all species)
- Pinks (*Dianthus*, all species)
- ○ Purple Coneflower (*Echinacea purpurea*)
- Scabiosa (*Scabiosa caucasica*)
- ○ Showy Stonecrop (*Sedum spectabile*)
- ○ Statice (*Limonium latifolium*)
- ○ Sunflower (*Helianthus*, all species)

Shade-Tolerant Plants for Woodland Understory

Small Trees

- Dogwood
  - Cornelian Cherry Dogwood (*Cornus mas*)
  - Flowering Dogwood (*Cornus florida*)
  - Kousa Dogwood (*Cornus kousa*)
- Eastern Hemlock (*Tsuga canadensis*)
- Holly
  - American Holly (*Ilex opaca*)
  - English Holly (*Ilex aquifolium*)
  - Longstalk Holly (*Ilex pedunculosa*)
- Japanese Maple (*Acer palmatum*)
- Japanese Privet (*Ligustrum japonicum*)
- Serviceberry
  - Allegheny Serviceberry (*Amelanchier laevis*)
  - Apple Serviceberry (*Amelanchier* x *grandiflora*)
  - Downy Serviceberry (*Amelanchier arborea*)

Shrubs

- Aromatic Sumac (*Rhus aromatica*)
- Boxwood (*Buxus*, all species)
- Cherry Laurel (*Prunus laurocerasus*)
- Dogwood
  - Bloodtwig Dogwood (*Cornus sanguinea*)

- Gray Dogwood (*Cornus racemosa*)
- Red Osier Dogwood (*Cornus sericea*)
- Silky Dogwood (*Cornus amomum*)
- Taterian Dogwood (*Cornus alba*)
- Elderberry (*Sambucus*, all species)
- Holly
  - Chinese Holly (*Ilex cornuta*)
  - Common Winterberry (*Ilex verticillata*)
  - Japanese Holly (*Ilex crenata*)
  - Possumhaw (*Ilex decidua*)
- Euonymus
  - Winged Euonymus (*Euonymus alatus*)
  - Wintercreeper (*Euonymus fortunei*)
- Privet
  - Amur Privet (*Ligustrum amurense*)
  - Border Privet (*Ligustrum obtusifolium*)
  - California Privet (*Ligustrum ovalifolium*)
- Serviceberry
  - Pacific Serviceberry (*Amelanchier florida*)
  - Running Serviceberry (*Amelanchier stolonifera*)
- Spicebush (*Lindera benzoin*)
- Viburnum
  - American Cranberrybush (*Viburnum triobum*)
  - Arrowwood Viburnum (*Viburnum dentatum*)
  - Hobblebush (*Viburnum alnifolium*)
  - Wayfaringtree Viburnum (*Viburnum lantana*)
- Witchhazel
  - Chinese Witchhazel (*Hamamelis mollis*)
  - Common Witchhazel (*Hamamelis virginiana*)
  - Japanese Witchhazel (*Hamamelis japonica*)
  - Vernal Witchhazel (*Hamamelis vernalis*)
- Yew (*Taxus*, all species)

Yellow Warbler on crab apple (Malus).

Plants for Small Places

(○ Good in containers)

Small Trees

Crab apple (*Malus*, all species)

Dogwood
  Cornelian Cherry Dogwood (*Cornus mas*)
  Flowering Dogwood (*Cornus florida*)

Hawthorn (*Crataegus*, all species)

Holly
  American Holly (*Ilex opaca*)
  English Holly (*Ilex aquifolium*)
  Longstalk Holly (*Ilex pedunculosa*)

Hornbeam (*Carpinus*, all species)

Maple
  Amur Maple (*Acer ginnala*)
  ○ Japanese Maple (*Acer palmatum*)

Serviceberry
  Allegheny Serviceberry (*Amelanchier laevis*)
  Apple Serviceberry (*Amelanchier x grandiflora*)
  Downy Serviceberry (*Amelchier arborea*)

Shrubs

○ Boxwood (*Boxus*, all species)

○ Cherry Laurel (*Prunus laurocerasus* 'Otto Luyken')

Firethorn (*Pyracantha* 'Lodense', 'Red Elf', and 'Tiny Tim')

Holly
  ○ Chinese Holly (*Ilex cornuta*)
  Common Winterberry (*Ilex verticillata*)
  ○ Japanese Holly (*Ilex crenata*)
  Possumhaw (*Ilex decidua*)
  ○ Yaupon (*Ilex vomitoria* 'Nana')

Honeysuckle
  Tatarian Honeysuckle (*Lonicera tatarica* 'Nana')
  European Fly Honeysuckle (*Lonicera x xylosteoides* 'Clavey's Dwarf' and 'Emerald Mound')

○ Juniper (*Juniperus*, all species)

○ Mugo Pine (*Pinus mugo* var. *mugo* 'Compacta')

Myrtle (*Myrtus communis*)

Serviceberry
  Pacific Serviceberry (*Amelanchier florida*)
  Running Serviceberry (*Amelanchier stolonifera*)

Shrub Bushclover (*Lespedeza bicolor*)

Vernal Witchhazel (*Hamamelis vernalis*)

Viburnum
  American Cranberrybush (*Viburnum trilobum* 'Compacta')
  European Cranberrybush (*Viburnum opulus* 'Compacta')

○ Yew (*Taxus*, all species, dwarf cultivars)

Fruiting Small Trees and Large Shrubs for Full Sun

Bayberry (*Myrica pensylvanica*)

Blackberry and Raspberry (*Rubus*, all species)

Blueberry (*Vaccinium*, all species)

Cherry and Plum (*Prunus*, all species)

Crab apple (*Malus*, all species)

Currant (*Ribes*, all species)

Dogwood
  Cornelian Cherry Dogwood (*Cornus mas*)
  Flowering Dogwood (*Cornus florida*)
  Kousa Dogwood (*Cornus kousa*)
  Red Osier Dogwood (*Cornus sericea*)

Elderberry (*Sambucus*, all species)

Elaeagnus (*Elaeagnus*, all species)

Firethorn (*Pyracantha*, all species)

Hawthorn (*Crataegus*, all species)

Holly
  American Holly (*Ilex opaca*)
  Chinese Holly (*Ilex cornuta*)
  Common Winterberry (*Ilex verticillata*)
  English Holly (*Ilex aquifolium*)
  Longstalk Holly (*Ilex pedunculosa*)
  Possumhaw (*Ilex decidua*)

Honeysuckle
  Amur Honeysuckle (*Lonicera maackii*)
  Morrow Honeysuckle (*Lonicera morrowii*)
  Tatarian Honeysuckle (*Lonicera tatarica*)

Winter Honeysuckle (*Lonicera fragantissima*)

Mountain Ash (*Sorbus*, all species)

Rose (*Rosa*, especially old-fashioned shrub types)

Sapphireberry (*Symplocos paniculata*)

Serviceberry (*Amelanchier*, all species)

Spicebush (*Lindera benzoin*)

Sumac (*Rhus*, all species)

Viburnum
  American Cranberrybush (*Viburnum trilobum*)
  Arrowwood Viburnum (*Viburnum dentatum*)
  Doublefile Viburnum (*Viburnum plicatum* var. *tomentosum*)
  European Cranberrybush (*Viburnum opulus*)
  Linden Viburnum (*Viburnum dilitatum*)
  Sargent Viburnum (*Viburnum sargentii*)
  Siebold Viburnum (*Viburnum sieboldii*)
  Tea Viburnum (*Viburnum setigerum*)

Fast-Growing Trees for Small Groves

Alder
  Black Alder (*Alnus glutinosa*)
  Italian Alder (*Alnus cordata*)

Birch (*Betula*, all species)

Eastern White Pine (*Pinus strobus*)

Green Ash (*Fraxinus pennsylvanica*)

Hackberry
  Common Hackberry (*Celtis occidentalis*)
  Sugar Hackberry (*Celtis laevigata*)

Honeylocust (*Gleditsia triacanthos*)

Oak
  Pin Oak (*Quercus palustris*)
  Red Oak (*Quercus rubra*)

Poplar, Aspen (*Populus*, all species)

Red Maple (*Acer rubrum*)

Sumac
  Flameleaf Sumac (*Rhus copallina*)
  Staghorn Sumac (*Rhus typhina*)

Sweet Gum (*Liquidambar styraciflua*)

Tuliptree (*Liriodendron tulipifera*)

Vines for the Garden

(○ Attaches to rough surfaces without a trellis)

Bittersweet
  American Bittersweet (*Celastrus scandens*)
  Oriental Bittersweet (*Celastrus orbiculatus*)

○ English Ivy (*Hedera helix*)

Fiveleaf Akebia (*Akebia quinata*)

Grape (*Vitis*, all species and cultivars)

Honeysuckle
  Everblooming Honeysuckle (*Lonicera x heckrottii*)
  Japanese Honeysuckle (*Lonicera japonica*)
  Trumpet Honeysuckle (*Lonicera sempervirens*)

Porcelain Ampelopsis (*Ampelopsis brevipedunculata*)

○ Virginia Creeper (*Parthenosis quinquefolia*)

○ Wintercreeper (*Euonymus fortunei*)

White-throated Sparrow on red maple in seed.

Shrubs for Hedges

Box Honeysuckle (*Lonicera nitida*)

Boxwood (*Boxus*, all species)

Cherry Laurel (*Prunus laurocerasus*)

Firethorn (*Pyracantha*, all species)

Holly
  Chinese Holly (*Ilex cornuta*)
  Japanese Holly (*Ilex crenata*)
  Yaupon (*Ilex vomitoria*)

Japanese Barberry (*Berberis thunbergii*)

Juniper (*Juniperus*, all species)

Myrtle (*Myrtus communis*)

Privet (*Ligustrum*, all species)

Silverberry (*Elaeagnus pungens*)

Wintercreeper (*Euonymus fortunei*)

Yew (*Taxus*, all species)

Favorite Landscape Plants Used by Common Birds for Food, Cover, and Nesting

These top favorites are the plants to add to attract birds to your garden. For further information on which species and varieties best fit your particular landscape, consult your local nursery and other books in the Ortho garden series.

- ● Food Only
- ★ Cover and Nesting Only
- ■ Food, Cover, and Nesting

Plant	American Goldfinch	American Robin	Black-capped Chickadee	Blue Jay	Brown Thrasher	Brown Towhee	Carolina Wren	Cedar Waxwing	Chipping Sparrow	Dark-eyed Junco	Downy Woodpecker	Eastern Bluebird	Eastern Phoebe	Evening Grosbeak	Gray Catbird	Hermit Thrush	House Finch	Mourning Dove	Northern Bobwhite
TREES																			
Alder	●		●														●	●	
Ash							●							●				●	
Beech			●	●						●								●	
Birch	●		■	●			●		●	★								●	
Crab Apple	●	■		■			●			●	★			●	■		●	●	
Elm	●	★	●							★				●				●	
Hackberry		●			●		●				●	●		●	●	●		●	
Hawthorn		■		■	■							●		■	●			●	
Hemlock	●	★	●	★					●			●					★		
Maple	■	■													■			●	
Mountain Ash							●					●		●				●	
Mulberry	●	●		●	●		●				●	●			●			●	
Oak		★		●	●	●				●							●	●	
Persimmon		●					●								●				
Pine	●	★	■	■	■		●	●	■	●				■		●	■	●	
Poplar			★								★			●					
Sassafras		●			●						●	●			●	●		●	
Spruce	●	★	■	★				●	★		■			■			■		
Sweet Gum	●		●			●				●							●	●	
Tupelo		●		●	●		●				●	●			●	●		●	
Walnut			●			●				●				●					
LARGE SHRUBS AND SMALL TREES																			
Buckthorn		●	●	●			●			●					●	●		●	
Cedar (Juniper)		■		■			■	★	●		●	●		■	●	●		●	
Cherry	●	●		●	●		●			●	●			●	●	●	●	●	
Dogwood	★	■		●			■			●	●			●	●	●	■	●	
Elaeagnus		●	●	●			●			●		●			●	●	■	●	
Holly		■	■	●			●			●		●		●	■	●	●	●	
Serviceberry	●	■		●			●			●	●	●		■	●	●	●		
Sumac		●		●	●	●				●	●	●			●	●		●	
LOW SHRUBS AND VINES																			
Barberry		●					●	★	●					■				●	
Bayberry			●	●		●				●	●	●			●	●		●	
Bittersweet		●					●				●				●			●	
Blackberry and Raspberry		●	●		■	●					●	●		●	●	●	●	●	
Blueberry		■	●								●	●		■	●			●	
Elderberry	★	●		●	■	●	●	●			●	●		■	●	●	●		
Firethorn		●		●	●						●			●	●			●	
Grape		●		●	■		●				●			■			●	●	
Honeysuckle	●	■			■		●		●		●			●	■			●	
Rose	●	●			■		●		●		●			●	■			●	
Spicebush		●												●	●				
Viburnum		●	■								●			■	●			●	
Virginia Creeper		●	●	●							●	●			●	●		●	

Northern Cardinal	Northern Flicker	Northern Mockingbird	Northern Oriole	Orchard Oriole	Pine Siskin	Purple Finch	Red-bellied Woodpecker	Red-eyed Vireo	Red-headed Woodpecker	Rose-breasted Grosbeak	Rufous-sided Towhee	Scarlet Tanager	Scrub Jay	Song Sparrow	Tree Swallow	Tufted Titmouse	White-breasted Nuthatch	White-crowned Sparrow	White-eyed Vireo	White-throated Sparrow	Wrentit	Wood Thrush	Yellow-bellied Sapsucker	Yellow-rumped Warbler	Yellow Warbler
				•	•					■			★												★
•					•																				
	•				•	•		•	•							•	•		•			•			
•		■			•	•			•							•						■			
•	•	■	■	■		•	•	★	•	•						•						•	•		
•	★		■		•	•	★	★		•							★					•	•	★	
•	•	•	•	•		•				•												•			
■	•	■																							
				•																	★				
•			★		•	•		★	★		■			•								•		★	
			•																						
•	•	•	•			•	•	•	•	•	•		•		•		•	•		•			•		
•	•		■			•		•	■	•	★	•			•	•				•					
■	•				■	■				•	•			•	•	•		•	•	★	•	■	★		
		■			•																■				
	•	•				•			•							•		•	•		★				
	★			■	■													•		■					
•			•	•						•					•	•		•							
	•	•		•	•	•	•		•					•						•					
•	•	■			•			•	•				•		•					•					
		•	•																	•	•				
■	•	■			•					•	★	•								•	•	•			
•	•	•	•	•	•	•	•	•	•	•	•	•	•		•			•		•	•			
•	•	•		■	•	■	•		■		•	•					•		■	•					
•	•	■		•	•			•		•	•			•	•				•						
■	•	•			•			•		•			■	■		•	•			•	■				
•	•	•		•	•	•		•	•	•							•					•			
•	•	•			•			•	•	•								•	•			•			
•					■								■												
	•	•				•				•	•		•	•		•	•		•			•			
•		•				•																			
■	•	■	•	•	•	•	•	•	•	•		•	•		•		■		•	•		•			
•	•	•			•	•	•	•	•	•		•	•			•		•		•		•			
•	•	■			•	•	•	•	•		•		•	•	•	•	•	•	•	•	•	•		★	
•	•			•		•	•	•			•				•					•					
■	•	■	•	•	•	•	•		•		•		•					•		•	•				
	•	■			•													•			•				
■		■										■								•					
•	•				•										•					•					
•	•	■			•										•		•			■					
	•	•				•	•			•				•	•	•	•			•	•	•			

Hummingbirds in the Garden

Their shining, jewellike colors and unique habits make hummingbirds among the most fascinating birds we can attract to our gardens. Their iridescent plumage comes in every hue—fiery red, glowing ruby, deep violet, metallic greens and blues, shimmering bronze, gold, and yellow, the colors changing with the bird's every movement and each shift of the light.

Everything about these tiny birds is interesting. With over 320 different species reported, they are one of the largest bird families. Most hummingbirds are concentrated in equatorial South America; only twelve species breed in North America, and most of those species are not widespread. Three of the most common species in the United States—the Anna's, Ruby-throated, and Rufous hummingbirds—are described in the "Gallery of Birds," pages 68–69. The plumage of all three of these species is basically green; even the gorget (throat area) of the male Ruby-throat appears green or black in the shade.

Despite their minute size, hummingbirds are extremely strong fliers. The Rufous Hummingbird is only about 3-1/2 inches long, and weighs about 1/9 ounce; yet it breeds as far north as southern Alaska and winters in Mexico—a migration of over 2000 miles. This migration takes place over several weeks, or even months, as the birds follow the blooming season of their favorite flowers. The even smaller (about 3-1/4 inches and 1/10 ounce) Ruby-throated Hummingbird migrates from as far north as southern Canada to as far south as Panama along a route that may cross the Gulf of Mexico—a nonstop flight of 500 miles. In preparation for its long trek the hummingbird stores up fat, increasing its body weight by as much as 50 percent.

Even when it's not migrating, the hummingbird needs to eat relatively huge quantities of food to fuel its rapid metabolism. In fact, ounce for ounce, hummingbirds require more calories than any other warm-blooded animal (except possibly for shrews), both to maintain their body temperature of about 105°F, and to fuel their extremely rapid movement. In forward flight, a hummingbird may beat its wings 75 times per second—no wonder we perceive them as a blur.

In flight, hummingbirds are uniquely adapted to gathering nectar from their favorite flowers. Not only can they hover motionless before a flower, they can dart backwards, up, down, in any direction, so quickly that they seem to vanish from sight. Many species of hummingbirds cannot walk at all. To shift positions on a branch, or to adjust her body on the nest, a hummingbird will simply rise in the air an inch or two, alighting again in a new position.

Feeding

Hummingbirds have two major sources of food: flower nectar, and tiny insects and spiders. They also frequently visit the holes that sapsuckers make in trees, both to drink the sweet sap and to snap up the insects that are also drawn by the sap. Although they visit nectar-bearing flowers of all colors, hummingbirds are most drawn to bright red, pink, and orange tubular flowers. The most important thing you can do to attract these birds to your garden is to plant flowering annuals, perennials, shrubs, and trees.

These birds will come eagerly to special feeders stocked with sugar water. The advantage of feeders is that they put the birds where you want them—close to the house or other places where they can be easily observed. Several models of hummingbird feeders are available. Bright red plastic flowers will guide the birds on their initial visits, although they will soon learn to seek out this rich food even if the location or appearance of the feeder is changed.

The formula for hummingbird food is simple: about one part white granulated

The hummingbird's long, slender bill and even longer, flexible tongue are supremely adapted for sipping nectar from the brightly colored tubular flowers that attract them. And the bird provides an equally important service for the plant—pollination. As it makes the rounds of the plants in its feeding territory, the bird's crown, bill, and throat are showered with pollen, which is transferred to the next flowers the bird visits. Below: Female Ruby-throated Hummingbird. Bottom: Hooded Oriole at hummingbird feeder.

sugar to four parts water. Boil the water, add the sugar, stir to dissolve thoroughly, and let the solution cool. Store unused solution in the refrigerator.

Fill the feeders daily. Every four or five days take them down and clean them thoroughly with hot water with a little vinegar added to prevent mold from becoming established. Scrub the feeders with a baby bottle brush, and rinse them thoroughly before refilling them.

Don't use honey solution in the feeders; it is a likely medium for the growth of a fungus that can infect the tongues of hummingbirds. And don't add red food coloring to the sugar solution, although the color is very attractive. Instead wrap the feeder with red plastic, ribbon, or tape.

The sweet, sticky sugar-water solution is also attractive to insects, including ants, flies, bees, and wasps. If ants find their way to the feeder, a generous application of salad oil or petroleum jelly on the wire from which the feeder hangs should prevent them from reaching the food. To discourage flying insects, try putting petroleum jelly around the feeder openings. You can also try repellant of the kind used to keep insects away from livestock; the offensive smell doesn't seem to bother the birds. Just don't apply the repellant where the birds' feet or bills can come in contact with it.

A temporary means of insect control is to turn a fine spray from a hose or sprinkler on the feeder. Insects are discouraged by the water; any sugar solution that has been dropped on the outside of the feeder is washed away; and hummingbirds love to flit in and out of the spray.

Many birds besides hummingbirds are attracted to these feeders, including some sparrows, chickadees, finches, nuthatches, orioles, and Downy Woodpeckers. If you want to offer sugar solution to birds other than hummingbirds, set up some feeders with perches for those birds that eat while perching, and reserve some feeders without perches for the hummingbirds, which feed while hovering.

Nesting

The nests of hummingbirds are so tiny—about the diameter of a half dollar—and so well camouflaged that they are seldom noticed. In most cases the male's responsibility ends when the eggs are fertilized. The female constructs her nest largely of plant down bound together with spider webs and saliva. The outside of the nest is camouflaged with bits of moss and lichen, so that it is virtually indistinguishable

from the branch to which it is attached. The eggs—usually two of them—are the size of a small bean. The mother incubates the eggs, without help from the male, for 15 to 19 days, depending on the species.

Newly hatched hummingbirds are almost completely featherless, and are remarkably ugly, but are more hardy than their size would indicate. The mother feeds them for about 25 days, by which time they leave the nest and begin to fend for themselves. Most hummingbirds raise two broods each breeding season.

Planting for Hummingbirds

Not only do flowers provide nectar, they also attract the tiny insects and spiders that are an important part of the hummingbird's diet. In the wild these birds prefer meadows, lowland forest edges, and woodland openings, especially near running water. To maximize the effect of plantings in your garden, plant flowers in clusters rather than scattering them about. Plant trumpet vines or honeysuckle on a trellis at the back of the garden, with groups of tall-growing flowers in front of it, ranging down to the shorter plants in the front of the beds, so that your view of your visitors will be unobstructed. An island of flowers or shrubbery in an expanse of lawn is also welcoming to hummingbirds. Even a window box or container plant with a mass of blooms is likely to attract a tiny guest.

Rufous Hummingbird feeding on winter currant (Ribes sanguineum).

Perhaps because they can so easily escape most kinds of danger, hummingbirds are curious and fearless little birds. They are quick to explore new sources of food, and the female is bold in defense of her nest, driving off intruders many times her size with repeated threatening dashes. Left: Anna's Hummingbird feeding young.

PROVIDING FOOD

Feeding birds all year round is easy and satisfying, if you know what kind of food each bird prefers, and how to present it.

A 1980 survey by the United States Department of the Interior reported that over sixty million people in the United States actively participate in feeding wild birds. That figure is rapidly growing, for good reason: feeding birds brings the beauty and wildness of nature up close, easily and with little expense. The variety of color and drama that the feeder concentrates just outside your window could scarcely be found in the wild. Children as well as adults are fascinated by watching birds at feeders. The interest of many professional naturalists was first sparked by such first-hand observation of how the natural world works.

A Year-Round Feeding Program

Although many people restrict their bird feeding to the cold, snowy winter months, it offers great fun and extra dividends when continued the year round. The warm months bring a different clientele to the feeder as migratory summer residents return from their southern ranges, and some winter visitors depart for their breeding places farther north. Birds tend to scatter at nesting time, becoming more territorial and less social, but the presence of a convenient food source can induce some to nest nearby. The dozen Northern Cardinals you might find at your feeder during the harshest days of winter will give way to a single breeding pair in spring and summer. It's especially satisfying to awake one morning and find a brood of young birds, newly flown from the nest, sampling food next to their parents at a feeder.

Even in the mild-winter areas of the Pacific Coast, Southwest, and Southeast, where many species remain throughout the year, summer feeding has its special pleasures. Many birds take on their most colorful plumage during the breeding season. The male American Goldfinch, for example, molts its drab olive winter feathers to reveal its brilliant yellow breeding plumage.

The summer feeding program should include most of the same foods offered in winter, with a few additions. Some summer visitors prefer special foods, such as fresh fruit for orioles and tanagers, or sugar solution for hummingbirds. Some foods that are excellent in cold weather spoil quickly in warm temperatures. Suet, for example, starts to melt and turn rancid at temperatures over 70°F. Special precautions must be taken if it is to be offered at all in the warm

Left: A male Northern Oriole finds an orange half a tasty treat. Right: Some birds, like this Blue Jay, are quite resourceful at finding food covered by snow. In general, however, food should be protected from bad weather, so that it is available when birds need it most.

months. Shelled nutmeats like peanuts or hulled sunflower seeds also spoil easily, and should be offered sparingly. Ground or cracked seeds and bakery products are especially vulnerable to spoilage if they get damp. All bird food, in fact, should be protected from moisture in both summer and winter.

Whether bird feeding is helpful or harmful to birds has been the subject of much debate. No scientific evidence supports the claim of some people that bird feeding affects the population of any species in any significant way, except to concentrate some birds locally where we want them, around our homes. Nature is simply too abundant with its resources, even in the harsh days of winter, to make any species as a whole count on us as its sole support. Neither is the claim substantiated by evidence that some species, like the Northern Cardinal, Tufted Titmouse, and Carolina Wren, are expanding their ranges farther north because of bird feeders. The Carolina Wren, for example, has been alternately wintering farther north in mild years and dying off in those areas in colder seasons, probably for thousands of years, and certainly long before bird feeding became popular.

Consistency in your bird feeding program is still a good idea, however, as it may be difficult to persuade birds to return to your feeding station if this resource proves unreliable. The possibility also exists that isolated individuals may come to rely on your handouts, neglecting their usual practice of scouting out a variety of more natural food sources. The best policy is not to interrupt your winter feeding program.

Along with consistency, cleanliness is important at the feeding station. Moldy, spoiled food can be dangerous to birds, and if it is left scattered about on the ground it can attract undesirable customers like rodents. Don't be overgenerous; set out only enough food so that it will all be eaten in a few days. Rake the ground beneath the feeders frequently to remove large leftovers and expose smaller pieces to the drying air. Occasionally clean off feeders that have become soiled in the scuffle and intensity of feeding. If you are attracting many ground-feeding birds, rotate the feeder so that debris doesn't concentrate in one spot.

Above left: Sunflower seeds are a special treat for cardinals. Top and above: An American Goldfinch uses a hanging globe feeder in much the same way it does a stalk of mullein.

Below: Evening Grosbeaks show little fear of hanging feeders, even when they are placed high off the ground.

Left: *A tube feeder is an economical way to provide more expensive seeds, in this case thistle and sunflower seeds for Pine Siskins.*

Below: *Nearly all birds will sample suet, even confirmed seedeaters like the Northern Cardinal.*

Bird Foods

The high-energy mainstays of any bird-feeding program are a source of fat, usually suet, and a selection of grains and seeds. Also necessary, and especially important in areas where snow covers up the natural supply, is grit. Birds have no teeth, and rely on the fine particles of grit in their gizzards to grind up hard seeds. Garden centers and feed stores sell grit that can be used for wild birds. It's usually composed of finely ground oyster shells, but any coarse sand will do. Scatter the grit on the feeding platform, or offer it in a shallow dish.

To suet, seed, grains, and grit a wide variety of foods may be added, including nutmeats, fresh, frozen, or dried fruits, nearly all baked goods, and certain kinds of table scraps. Peanut butter mix is considered by many people to be an essential ingredient in any bird-feeding program, both because birds love it and because it is a convenient way to provide high-quality protein and fat. Except for suet and composite blocks designed to be pecked, and some fruits, all foods presented to birds should be offered in tiny bite-size pieces.

Suet

Suet (beef or mutton fat) is the tastiest, least expensive, and most readily available source of animal fats for birds. It is popular with nearly all birds in winter, especially when mixed with seeds and other tidbits. Suet begins to melt at about 70°F and quickly turns rancid, so it should be offered with caution during warm weather.

Other Fats and Meat

Bacon drippings, shortening, and meat fats rendered from cooking (as long as they are not heavily spiced) can be used in place of, or in addition to, suet. Other sources of fats and proteins include cheese (American cheese is best, followed by cottage and cream cheese); butter; buttermilk (milk sours too quickly); meat scraps (cut in tiny chunks and not highly spiced); bacon scraps; finely ground or diced raw meat; crumbled dry dog food and dog biscuits moistened with water; and canned dog food. Robins and other insect-eating birds will appreciate a bone with scraps of meat on it.

Seeds

Many excellent wild birdseed mixtures are available from garden centers, nurseries, feed stores, bird clubs, and grocery stores, as well as mail order outlets. Two old-fashioned mixes, chick feed and scratch feed, are available in feed stores. However, some commercial mixtures contain substantial amounts of inexpensive seeds that are likely to be ignored by the birds at your feeder. You may find it more satisfying to make your own mixture from bulk seed. This has the advantage of being tailored to the individual needs of the birds you want to attract (or *not* attract).

The best way to formulate your own mixture is by using a testing tray (see illustration on page 43). This tray is easy to make, and is composed of a number of separate compartments, one for each kind of seed tested. Label each compartment with the kind of seed it contains, place the tray at your feeding station, and keep a careful record at the end of each day of the amounts of seed eaten. Two or three weeks of testing will give you an idea of the relative proportions of the various seeds you should add to a mixture that is tailored to the preferences of the birds in your area. You may want to continue this test throughout the feeding season, however, as preferences and bird populations may change. In the recipe section we offer a recommended seed mixture that is useful in most areas. The chart on page 41 gives the food preference of the most common seedeating birds.

Fruits

Fruits and berries, fresh, dried, or frozen, are an important part of the summer feeding program, and birds like orioles and tanagers may be attracted by little else.

Fruits should be chopped into tiny bite-size pieces before being offered. An exception is fresh coconut, which can be a wonderful bird food served in the shell. Larger pieces of fruit, such as bananas and apple and orange halves, may be secured to the feeding platform so that birds can't carry them off.

Fruits especially loved by birds include apples (raw or baked), apricots, bananas, blueberries, cherries (wild or domestic), cranberries (raw, frozen, relish, or jelly), currants (fresh or dried), dates, crab apples, prunes, figs, grapes (raw and sliced, especially white seedless), loquats, oranges, peaches, pears, raisins, strawberries, and watermelon.

Peanut Butter

Mixed with such things as corn meal and suet, peanut butter is a relatively inexpensive way to offer high-protein foods to birds, as well as high-energy fats, and is an excellent substitute for the far more expensive nutmeats. Protein in general is scarce for birds in the winter. Fortunately, their protein requirements are much less during the cold months than when they are growing, molting, or reproducing.

Nuts

Nuts are high in protein, fats, and minerals, and are an excellent bird food. Their chief disadvantage is that they are expensive; they can be considered only as luxury items at the bird table, as special treats.

Nuts should generally be served out of the shell and broken into small pieces. Pecans and walnuts can be halved and served in the shell; birds will pick out the meats more efficiently than you can. Like corn and sunflower seeds, nuts are also a favorite of squirrels and other rodents.

Above: *Mockingbirds are attracted by little else than dried fruit at the bird feeder. This Connecticut resident eats raisins in winter.* Left: *Pine cones make excellent natural feeders to present peanut butter. This one, being visited by a House Finch, shows evidence of an earlier squirrel raid.*

Attractiveness of Birdseeds to Common Birds

	Buckwheat	Canary Seed	Crack Corn—fine	Flax Seed	Millet—German ("Golden")	Millet—Red Proso	Millet—White Prose ("White")	Milo (Sorghum)	Oats—Hulled (Groats)	Oats (Whole)	Peanut—Hearts	Peanut—Kernels	Rice	Rape Seed	Safflower Seed	Sunflower—Black oil type	Sunflower—Black-striped	Sunflower—Grey-striped	Sunflower—Hulled	Thistle (Niger)	Wheat
American Goldfinch (s)	L	L	L	L	L	L	L	L	L	L	L	L	L	L	L	H	H	M	H	H	L
Blue Jay (s)	L	L	M	L	L	L	L	L	L	L	L	L	H	L	L	L	M	H	H	L	L
Chickadee (s)	L	L	L	L	L	L	L	L	L	L	L	L	M	L	L	L	H	H	H	M	L
Common Grackle (s)	L	L	H	L	L	L	L	L	L	M	M	M	L	L	L	H	H	H	H	L	L
Evening Grosbeak (s)	L	L	L	L	L	L	L	L	L	L	L	L	L	L	L	H	H	H	M	L	L
House Finch (s)	L	M	L	M	L	L	M	L	L	L	M	M	L	M	L	H	H	M	H	H	M
House Sparrow (p)	L	M	M	L	M	M	H	L	L	L	L	L	L	L	L	M	M	M	M	L	M
Mourning Dove (p)	M	H	M	L	H	H	H	M	L	L	M	L	L	L	M	H	M	M	M	M	M
Northern Cardinal (s)	L	L	L	L	L	L	M	L	L	L	L	L	L	L	M	H	H	H	M	L	L
Purple Finch (s)	L	M	L	L	L	L	L	L	L	L	L	L	L	L	L	H	H	H	M	M	L
Scrub Jay (s)	L	L	L	L	L	L	L	L	L	L	L	L	H	L	L	L	H	H	H	L	L
Song Sparrow (p)	L	H	L	L	H	H	H	L	L	L	M	L	L	L	M	M	M	M	M	L	L
Tufted Titmouse (s)	L	L	L	L	L	L	L	L	L	L	L	H	L	L	L	H	H	H	L	L	L
White-crowned Sparrow (p)	L	M	M	M	M	H	H	M	L	M	H	H	L	L	L	H	H	M	H	L	L
White-throated Sparrow (p)	L	M	H	L	H	H	H	M	M	M	M	H	L	L	M	H	H	M	H	L	M

KEY:
H = High attractiveness relative to standard feed (more than 50 percent as attractive)
M = Moderate attractiveness relative to standard feed (from 15 to 50 percent as attractive)
L = Low attractiveness relative to standard feed (less than 15 percent as attractive)
s = Black-striped sunflower seed used as standard feed
p = White proso millet used as standard feed

In the past, bird feeding recommendations have been riddled with myths, suppositions, and unsupported claims, but thanks to the work of Dr. A. D. Geis of the United States Fish and Wildlife Service we now have solid information on the seed preferences of wild birds common at bird feeders. First limited to Maryland, Dr. Geis' research soon expanded to Maine, Ohio, and California, to show that the seed preferences of the bird species studied were remarkably similar across the nation. The information on seedeating birds in this chapter is based on that research.

Each of the seeds on this chart was compared with two "standard" seeds to determine which was preferred by birds commonly found at feeding stations. The standard seeds—black-striped sunflower seed and white proso millet—were selected on the basis of preliminary observations indicating that of the seeds commonly fed to birds, these two are the most generally attractive to the most species.

The breakdown of preferences given in this chart is general, and is intended only to guide you in selecting seeds to attract those birds you specifically want to feed.

Baked Goods

Quite a bit of debate centers around the nutritional value of baked goods for birds. There is little question, however, that birds love bakery products, especially pie crusts, doughnuts, fried breads and pancakes, and greasy crusts high in fats. White bread crumbs are the best way to get birds to notice your feeder, and are excellent for getting things started in the fall. Whole and cracked wheat products, bread, cake, and cracker crumbs, cooked cereals, and cooked spaghetti and noodles chopped in small pieces are well received. Cornbread, cornmeal, mush, grits, and other corn products are also popular. Disadvantages are that baked goods quickly become moldy, and may cause disease. They are also particularly attractive to starlings and House Sparrows.

Recipes

These basic recipes are designed to appeal to the widest variety of birds across the country. A little experimentation will soon show which of these treats appeal to your particular birds.

Recommended Birdseed Mix

Many birdseed mixes are available commercially. If you decide to make your own mix, this simple recipe should appeal to a wide variety of seed-eating birds.

Sunflower Seeds (unhulled oil type)	50%
Millet (white proso)	35%
Cracked corn (fine or medium)	15%

Preparing Suet

Beef suet is preferred above other kinds, and can be purchased cheaply from the butcher. Be sure to ask for "short" suet or kidney suet rather than "stringy" suet, and make sure that it is fresh, firm, and white. If you plan on melting it down, ask your butcher to grind it for you. Or you can grind it yourself with a kitchen grinder.

Heat the ground suet in a double boiler, or in a small saucepan placed inside a larger pan of boiling water, until it has been rendered to a liquid state. Allow hot suet to cool and thicken before adding seeds; otherwise they will float to the top. A wide variety of seeds, fruits, and other bird treats can be stirred into the thickening suet before pouring it into forms or packing it into bird feeders.

An alternate procedure is to heat the ground suet as described above, then allow it to cool and solidify. Remove the solidified fat that has risen to the surface and let it drain. This purified fat can be stored in the refrigerator, or reheated and made into suet-seed cakes immediately. Purified and reheated suet makes harder cakes when cooled a second time, and will last much longer outdoors. This is an essential procedure when offering suet in the spring and summer.

Commercial suet-seed cakes are widely available, and most have the advantage of being highly refined and very hard, retarding spoilage. They also fit neatly into commercial suet feeders. Many birds prefer the softer homemade mixtures, however, and the special treats you add to them.

High Protein Suet Mix for Insect-Eating Birds

4-1/2 cups ground fresh suet
3/4 cup dried and finely ground bakery goods (whole or cracked wheat bread and crackers are best)
1/2 cup hulled, raw, and unsalted sunflower seed
1/4 cup millet (white proso is best)
1/4 cup dried and chopped berries (currants, raisins, or dried wild berries)
3/4 cup dried and finely ground meat (optional)

1. *Melt suet in a saucepan.*
2. *Mix together the rest of the ingredients in a large mixing bowl.*
3. *Allow suet to cool until slightly thickened, then add it to the mixture in the bowl. Mix well.*
4. *Pour or pack into forms or suet feeders; smear onto tree trunks or overhanging limbs and branches; or pack into pine cones.*

Suet Tidbit Cakes

1/2 pound fresh ground suet
1/8 cup canary seed
1/8 cup chopped peanuts
1/4 cup raisins or currants
1/8 cup cooked oatmeal
1/8 cup cooked rice
1/4 cup sunflower seeds
1/4 cup fine cracked corn

1. *Melt suet in a saucepan.*
2. *Mix together the rest of the ingredients in a large mixing bowl.*
3. *Allow melted suet to cool until it starts to thicken, then add dry mix and stir until evenly distributed.*
4. *Pour into pie pan or form, or pack into suet feeders.*

Many variations are possible with this mixture. Other ingredients worth including are millet or other birdseed, cornmeal, cooked noodles or spaghetti, chopped berries, and dried fruits of all kinds. You can experiment to see which proportions your birds like best.

Black-capped Chickadee.

Soft Peanut Butter Mix

Relished by a wide variety of birds, this mix is great for packing into feeders or smearing on tree trunks.

1 cup freshly ground suet
1 cup peanut butter
3 cups yellow cornmeal
1/2 cup enriched white or whole wheat flour

1. *Melt suet in a saucepan.*
2. *Add peanut butter, stirring until melted and well blended.*
3. *In a separate bowl, mix together the last two ingredients.*
4. *After suet-peanut butter blend has cooled and started to thicken, add dry mixture and blend into dough. It is now ready to serve.*

Hard Peanut Butter Mix

This mixture will last longer out of doors than will the soft mixture.

2 cups suet
1 cup peanut butter
2 cups yellow cornmeal
2 cups fine cracked corn

1. *Melt the suet, allow it to cool thoroughly, and reheat it.*
2. *Add peanut butter, stirring until melted and well blended.*
3. *Add dry ingredients to liquid and blend well.*
4. *Pour into forms or suet feeders and cool until hardened.*

Presenting Food

How food is presented to birds is nearly as important as the type of food offered. Much thought and consideration should be devoted to the presentation of bird food; you will find a flexible, experimental attitude quite rewarding. Try several approaches in order to find the one favored by the birds in your area.

Many styles and forms of seed feeders and suet feeders are commercially available. The illustrations on pages 44 and 45 show some of these, along with some birds that they attract. Also illustrated is a plan for a bird feeder that you can make. The chart on page 46 will help you decide which type of feeder you should buy if you have specific birds in mind.

o The feeder should manipulate birds so you can see them. The type of feeder you choose will determine where you can place it. However, visibility should not be the only criterion for placing your bird feeders. Some of the more cautious birds may never come to your feeders at all if they are too close to the house.
o The feeder should be designed for the type of food you plan to offer. Thistle seed and suet are best offered in special feeders, for example. Chopped table scraps and fruit cannot be presented if you have only a hopper-type feeder for birdseed.
o The feeder should dispense food as it is needed by the birds. This can be an advantage with some kinds of birds, a disadvantage with others. For example, a cardinal hunting for sunflower seeds may quickly empty and scratch away mixed birdseed from a hopper feeder. The sunflower seeds may need to be presented alone in a separate feeder. Self-dispensing suet feeders should be mounted at a downward tilt so that the suet falls against the screen or netting through which the birds peck.
o The feeder should protect food from the weather. Rain and dampness can quickly spoil birdseed, particularly cracked cereal grains. Food covered by snow is difficult for birds to notice and reach at a time when they need it the most.
o The feeder and its placement should help prevent attacks from predators and food raids by other less desirable creatures, such as rats and mice. Ground feeders are particularly vulnerable to raids by unwanted visitors.

Some Ground and Platform Feeders

Many birds prefer to feed at ground level, and even with elevated feeders much of the activity occurs on the ground underneath, where leftovers have been dropped. Rather than scattering food on the bare ground, use a large piece of marine plywood as a floor. It's easy to keep clean by hosing off. Or raise the feeder a few inches off the ground, as shown. In its basic version a platform feeder is simply a flat tray elevated 5 to 8 feet above the ground on a pole or post, suspended by wire from an overhead support like an eave or a tree limb, or attached to a windowsill. A lip of narrow strips of wood, glued or tacked around the perimeter, will prevent food from spilling or blowing out, and provides a perch for small birds. Leave a 1-inch space at each corner of this lip for drainage, and to make cleaning easier.

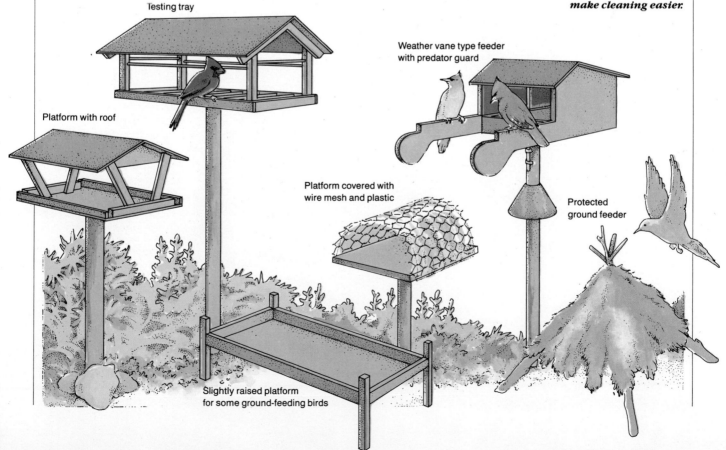

Testing tray

Platform with roof

Weather vane type feeder with predator guard

Platform covered with wire mesh and plastic

Protected ground feeder

Slightly raised platform for some ground-feeding birds

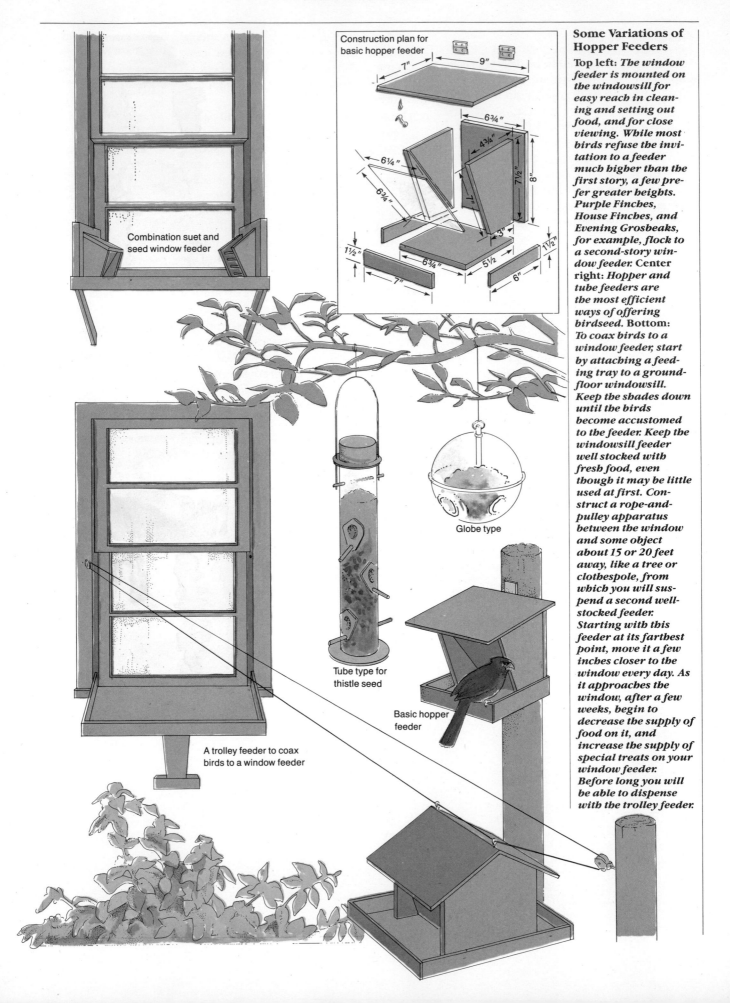

Combination suet and seed window feeder

Construction plan for basic hopper feeder

7" 9"

6¾"

4¾"

6¼"

6¾"

7"

7½"

8"

3"

1½"

6¾"

7"

5½"

6"

1½"

Globe type

Tube type for thistle seed

Basic hopper feeder

A trolley feeder to coax birds to a window feeder

Some Variations of Hopper Feeders

Top left: *The window feeder is mounted on the windowsill for easy reach in cleaning and setting out food, and for close viewing. While most birds refuse the invitation to a feeder much higher than the first story, a few prefer greater heights. Purple Finches, House Finches, and Evening Grosbeaks, for example, flock to a second-story window feeder. Center right: Hopper and tube feeders are the most efficient ways of offering birdseed. Bottom: To coax birds to a window feeder, start by attaching a feeding tray to a ground-floor windowsill. Keep the shades down until the birds become accustomed to the feeder. Keep the windowsill feeder well stocked with fresh food, even though it may be little used at first. Construct a rope-and-pulley apparatus between the window and some object about 15 or 20 feet away, like a tree or clothespole, from which you will suspend a second well-stocked feeder. Starting with this feeder at its farthest point, move it a few inches closer to the window every day. As it approaches the window, after a few weeks, begin to decrease the supply of food on it, and increase the supply of special treats on your window feeder. Before long you will be able to dispense with the trolley feeder.*

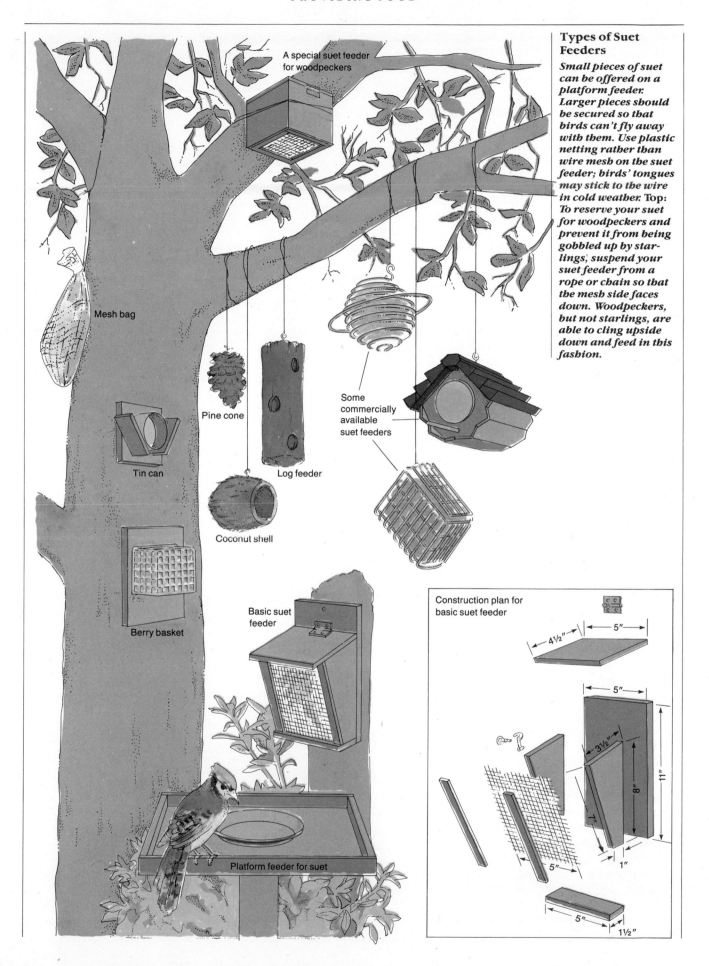

A special suet feeder for woodpeckers

Mesh bag

Tin can

Pine cone

Log feeder

Coconut shell

Berry basket

Basic suet feeder

Platform feeder for suet

Some commercially available suet feeders

Types of Suet Feeders

Small pieces of suet can be offered on a platform feeder. Larger pieces should be secured so that birds can't fly away with them. Use plastic netting rather than wire mesh on the suet feeder; birds' tongues may stick to the wire in cold weather. Top: To reserve your suet for woodpeckers and prevent it from being gobbled up by starlings, suspend your suet feeder from a rope or chain so that the mesh side faces down. Woodpeckers, but not starlings, are able to cling upside down and feed in this fashion.

Construction plan for basic suet feeder

4½" 5"

5"

3½"

11"

8"

7"

1"

5"

5"

1½"

Location of Bird Feeders

The best way to determine where most birds prefer to have their dinner in your yard is by experimenting. Remember, though, that birds are creatures of habit and do not respond well to abrupt and radical changes in the position of feeders. Use the following criteria to determine the spots you should try first.

o A wide variety of feeding spots and types of feeders is important. For example, different birds like to feed at different heights. A well-rounded program would include some ground feeding; a platform feeder on a post about 5 feet off the ground; a few hopper or tube feeders for individual types of seeds, suspended by wires at about 5 to 8 feet high; a thistle feeder; a window feeder; and some suet feeders mounted on tree trunks at various heights.

o Birds also appreciate a variety of feeder placement with respect to surrounding vegetation. If you have the space, consider establishing two or three feeding stations, spaced about 50 feet apart, each with a variety of feeders at different heights. This can be effective for two reasons. First, it allows you to cater to the preferences of different bird species by taking advantage of the different types of plant groupings you might have in your yard, such as open space, an area close to shrubs and small trees, or a dense woodland. Second, it will solve many problems of unruly behavior; the irritable individual that chases other birds off will be less able to defend several feeding areas. Wary flocks of aggressive birds, like starlings, can be diverted with cheap foods like breadcrumbs, dogfood, and table scraps to stations more distant from the house.

o Consider the many natural "platform feeders" you may have on your property, such as tree stumps, flat rocks, and the tops of walls and fenceposts.

o Especially in winter, birds favor the most sheltered locations. Besides being uncomfortable for birds, strong winds can cause hanging feeders to move excessively and to scatter the food. The south side of the house is generally the warmest, and areas buffered by trees and shrubs also have milder microclimates.

Common and Occasional Winter-feeding Birds and the Types of Feeders They Prefer

	Ground Feeders	Raised Feeders, Low	Raised Feeders, High	Hanging Feeders (Seed)	Hanging Feeders (Suet)	Tree Trunk (Suet, Seed Cakes)
COMMON WINTER FEEDERS						
American Goldfinch		●		●		
American Tree Sparrow	●	●				
Black-capped Chickadee	●	●		●		
Blue Jay		●	●			
Common Grackle	●	●				
Dark-eyed Junco	●	●				
Downy Woodpecker		●			●	●
Evening Grosbeak			●			
House Finch		●		●		
House Sparrow	●	●				
Mourning Dove	●					
Northern Cardinal		●				
Northern Flicker	●	●			●	●
Northern Mockingbird		●				
Pine Siskin		●	●			
Purple Finch		●	●			
Red-bellied Woodpecker	●	●			●	●
Red-breasted Nuthatch	●	●			●	●
Red-headed Woodpecker	●	●			●	●
Red-winged Blackbird	●	●				
Song Sparrow	●	●				
Starling	●	●		●		
Tufted Titmouse		●		●		
White-breasted Nuthatch		●			●	●
White-crowned Sparrow	●	●				
White-throated Sparrow	●	●				
Yellow-bellied Sapsucker		●			●	●
OCCASIONAL WINTER FEEDERS						
Brown Thrasher	●	●				
Carolina Wren		●				
Chipping Sparrow	●	●				
Hermit Thrush	●	●				
House Wren		●				
Northern Oriole		●				
Rufous-sided Towhee	●					
Wood Thrush	●	●				

Protecting the Feeder

Feeding stations aren't attractive just to the birds you want to enjoy. Unwelcome guests at the banquet you offer may include squirrels and nuisance birds like starlings. Besides protecting the food you set out from these raiders, you may need to protect your visitors as well, from predatory cats.

Nuisance Birds

Both European Starlings and House Sparrows seem to prefer ground feeding, and selecting a spot well away from the house to scatter their preferred foods will do much to free your closer feeders for more desirable visitors.

Although they are not particularly shy around human dwellings, House Sparrows tend to avoid hanging, wobbly feeders that move about in the wind. Their favorite foods are bread crumbs and related bakery products, cracked corn and wheat, and kitchen scraps. Use these less expensive foods to divert them to other parts of the yard. Neither starlings nor House Sparrows will eat whole kernels of corn.

Unlike House Sparrows, starlings will frequent nearly any type of feeder, and even learn to cling to hanging plastic mesh bags of suet. Unlike woodpeckers, nuthatches, and creepers, however, they are unable to cling upside down; they can't get at suet feeders suspended so that the only exposed part is facing down.

Unlike most other birds, starlings tend to feed late in the morning and early in the afternoon, so offering food early and late in the day can give the more desirable species a head start on their share. Starlings also shun hard-coated seeds like sunflowers, whole-kernel corn, and peanuts in the shell, and hard, twice-melted suet mixed with seed. They are particularly fond of table scraps and dogfood (both canned and dry), and these can be used to divert their activity away from choicer feeding stations.

Squirrels

Although the antics of squirrels are fascinating to watch, they can be a considerable nuisance around bird feeders, eating a great deal of food and scaring away songbirds. If squirrels are a problem in your yard, there are some steps you can take to prevent them from reaching the feeder.

Feeders should be elevated at least 5 feet off the ground, as squirrels are excellent jumpers. They should be placed 8 to 10 feet away from the nearest building, tree, or overhanging branch for the same reason. Squirrels can be discouraged from running down wires or jumping onto hanging feeders by stringing a series of pie pans or smooth sheet metal discs with a hole punched in the center along the wire. The discs tip to dump the squirrels off. Separate the discs with short lengths of old garden hose. Feeders mounted on posts can be squirrel-proofed by fastening a smooth, metal, funnel-shaped collar around the post at least 4 feet up from the ground. Above this funnel, fasten a tight band of sheet metal around the post that spans a distance of at least 18 inches (see the weather vane feeder on page 43). These prevent the squirrel from gripping anything.

Cats

If cats harrass the birds in your garden, be sure to place bird feeders well off the ground and at least 15 feet from shrubbery and other hiding places. Trim any over hanging limbs from which they may pounce. A cat out in the open is rarely successful in catching a bird, although it will make them skittish and perhaps even drive them away altogether. If the cat is yours, keep it inside during the day, particularly at those times when birds are in the habit of feeding. Hanging a bell around the cat's neck will help alert birds to its presence, but it will do little to reduce their shyness and fear.

Squirrels are clever and unrelenting in their raids on bird feeders.

PROVIDING WATER

Water—in a fountain, pool, or birdbath—is as irresistable to birds as it is to people. Here are easy ways to provide fresh water in your garden all year round.

A reliable source of fresh water is an essential ingredient in any bird-attracting program. Many species of birds that don't eat the specialized foods we provide may be drawn to the garden by water. In the arid Southwest water is a scarce resource for birds, and the most important thing we can offer to attract them to the garden. Even in the moist Northeast and Northwest, water in the form birds prefer can be hard to find. Especially during long dry spells, and in winter when water is frozen, birds may have a long search for a chance to drink and bathe.

There are many ways to provide water for birds while enhancing the beauty of the garden at the same time. The artificial "rain puddles" we call birdbaths are available in a huge variety of sizes, forms, and materials. If you have a garden pool, it can be adapted to the special needs of birds. If you're starting from scratch, a simple pool is easily constructed. A plastic tub, old wine barrel or bathtub, a scooped-out log, a simple hole in the ground lined with plastic, or a garden hose with a mist spray can entice birds to use the water you provide.

Fresh Water Year Round

However you present it, water should be fresh, clean, and abundant. Birdbaths should be hosed off and refilled often, and checked daily in hot weather. Garden pools should be periodically cleaned out and refilled. A recirculating pump and the cooperation of fish and plants will help keep the water fresh and clear. Water intended for birds is no place for chemicals of any kind. Never add chemicals to it to control algae or insects, or to prevent freezing. Be sure that spray drift or runoff from chemicals and fertilizer you use in the garden doesn't get in the water. Don't use lead-lined birdbaths and plumbing fixtures, as lead can poison birds.

Water should be available and accessible in all seasons. One of the prime attractions of water you provide is its reliability; natural sources tend to shift, dry up, or freeze with changing weather. The birdbath is popular even in the coldest days of winter, and it's important to keep it unfrozen. Birdbaths and very small pools can be thawed by pouring a kettle of boiling water in them, but this is tedious to do on a regular basis.

The most convenient way to keep the water from freezing is to use an immersion water heater designed specifically for outdoor use, like the one illustrated on page 52. Several varieties are available in garden stores and hardware centers. Some

Water is an irresistable enticement to birds, whether it's gently flowing into a basin (opposite page, with Blue Jay), or in a garden birdbath raised on a pedestal (right, with American Robin).

are designed for water deeper than that usually found in birdbaths and are more appropriate for pools and tubs in the garden. For the shallow water of a birdbath or small garden pool, purchase the smaller version, designed to operate at a depth of 1-1/2 to 3 inches. Either type should have an automatic thermostat that shuts the heating element off when the water reaches 40°F. If an extension cord is needed, be sure to use the heavy-duty exterior kind with a triple-pronged, grounded plug. Special heating tapes are available for use in birdbaths, but are appropriate to use only in mild climates with occasional freezes.

Making Water Accessible

The surface where birds enter the water should be rough to provide sure footing. Textured materials appropriate for birdbaths, pools, and streams include concrete, stone, pebbles, and sand. Smooth, slippery surfaces like plastic or metal can be made more attractive to birds by roughening them with coarse sandpaper or attaching the kind of textured footing used on the bottom of bathtubs.

The water container should have a gradual, shallow approach. Almost all garden birds are fearful of water deeper than 2 or at most 3 inches, and some like it even shallower than that. Don't buy a birdbath any deeper than 3 inches, and do select one that approaches this depth very gradually.

*Above left: **Blue Jays are especially fond of birdbaths**, not only for drinking but for energetic bathing as well. Above right: **The Northern Flicker**, like other woodpeckers, appears to draw water through its bill like a straw. Actually it is lapping it up by extending and retracting its brushlike tongue.*

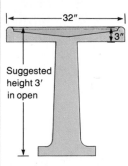

The dimensions and placement of a birdbath are crucial. The basin should be 24 to 36 inches in diameter, gradually sloping to a depth of no more than 3 inches at the deepest point. If the birdbath is placed in the open, the pedestal should be at least 3 feet in height for protection from predators.

The depth should increase 1 inch over a space of 8 inches. A lip or other perch where birds can alight before entering the water is an advantage, as is a dry flat space on which they can hop to the water's edge.

Many garden pools have an abrupt edge, so that the water is immediately too deep. Place a large rock in the water so that birds can alight on the exposed top. For clinging birds, place a flower pot upside down in the pool and insert a twiggy branch in the hole of the pot. Small birds will land on lily pads for a drink and a quick splash.

Placing Water for Safety and Viewing

Safety is a prime consideration in locating the water source. A wet bird, preoccupied with bathing and slowed down by wet feathers, is a vulnerable target for cats. The water source should be out in the open, with no close shrubs behind which a predatory cat can lurk or overhanging limbs it can pounce from. Most birds prefer a high perch and dense cover about 15 feet away from the water so that they can examine the area for possible danger and return to their refuge for preening. A few birds, however, especially birds of the forest floor like thrushes, prefer secret forest pools and quiet streams that are close to cover. These shy birds are more likely to visit a birdbath or garden pool hidden in dense shrubbery.

Height gives added protection to birds.

Left: *A concrete bird-bath provides this House Finch with nonslip footing. The gradually sloping depth and lip for perching are further hallmarks of a good birdbath.* Above: *Birds can be re-sourceful in finding water. This Gila Woodpecker in Tucson, Arizona enjoys a modern water source.*

If your birdbath is near dense vegetation, it's especially important to raise it off the ground about 3 feet. Out in the open, ground-level birdbaths and pools are acceptable. A cat that is exposed rarely gets close enough to be a threat to birds.

Water should also be located in a spot that is convenient for you to enjoy the visitors it attracts. Locate your water source near a place you use a lot, like the house, patio, or quiet sitting area. Don't mask your line of sight with dense vegetation. Water for the birds should be located as close to a faucet as possible, so you don't have to lug long, heavy coils of hose for cleaning and refilling.

Ways to Supply Water

How you decide to provide water for birds will depend on the time and expense you wish to spend rigging the method up, the time you are willing to devote to maintenance, and what you find appropriate and beautiful for your garden.

Birdbaths

A birdbath is the easiest way to set up a water source for birds in the garden. Birdbaths are available in a variety of ornamental styles, from simple, naturalistic ones of stone or wood to colorful, elaborate sculptures. Don't buy a birdbath with

This garden pool at the base of a tree is made to order for White-throated Sparrows.

any moving, shiny objects that might frighten birds. Otherwise, don't hesitate to give your esthetic sense free reign.

Many different types of support are available. Some birdbaths are simple dishes to set on the ground, or on a windowsill or deck. Some are made to hang by chains from a balcony, eave, or wall bracket, or to attach to a window with suction cups. The most common type is set on a pedestal, raised 3 feet off the ground. Heavy stone, ceramic, or concrete dishes should have a broad, sturdy support. Lighter metal, plastic, or wooden birdbaths should be firmly anchored to the pedestal or be of single-piece construction.

As long as its edge slopes gradually, the size of the basin is not crucial. However, anything less than 12 inches across is generally too small, and baths or pools 18 inches in diameter or less will usually be used by only one bird at a time. Most birdbaths are 24 to 36 inches in diameter, and this seems to be a good size even for community bathing.

Birdbaths are available in a wide variety of materials. Terra-cotta and glazed ce-

Immersion Heater

An immersion water heater will keep the water in your birdbath thawed out and accessible all winter. Be sure the one you buy is designed to operate at a depth of 1½ to 3 inches.

Some Commercially Available Birdbaths

The simplest way to offer water in your garden is in a birdbath. The ones shown here are made from readily available materials.

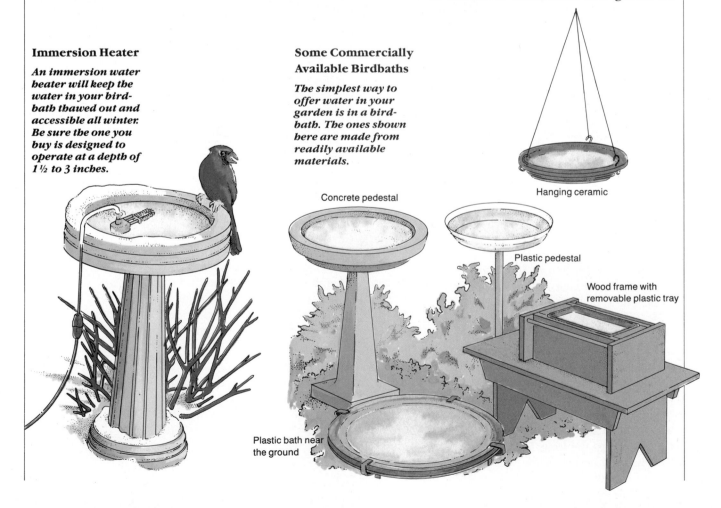

Hanging ceramic

Concrete pedestal

Plastic pedestal

Wood frame with removable plastic tray

Plastic bath near the ground

ramic birdbaths are attractive, but crack easily when water freezes in winter. Concrete and cement birdbaths are the most commonly available, and their rough texture is a decided advantage. The solid, heavy construction of concrete withstands freezing better than terra-cotta, glazed ceramic, or cement. (Cement is concrete without reinforcing gravel.) But, to be safe, all kinds should be emptied before cold weather, unless you take measures to ensure that the water will never freeze.

Plastic and metal birdbaths withstand all kinds of weather, but these surfaces are too slippery unless the surface is textured. Their light weight makes them easy to handle, but requires a firm, solid support to keep them from tipping. Metal birdbaths should be made of stainless steel or coated with rust-resistant paint. Painted metal birdbaths will eventually chip and flake, and will need occasional repainting.

A few birdbaths sold commercially are made entirely of wood. They are more difficult to keep clean, and even those made from long-lasting wood, like redwood or cedar, won't last as long as other kinds of birdbaths. They are generally well liked by birds, however, and can be very attractive.

With a little imagination you can easily make your own birdbath. Any kind of dish with a gradual slope, lip for perching, and appropriate depth and dimensions can be used. The kind of saucer usually placed under large potted plants can make an excellent tiny birdbath. A 3-foot log, cut square on both ends, makes a good pedestal. A close-grained log like oak or hickory can be hollowed out with a chisel to contain water. A large stone from a creek bed that has a natural depression on top to hold water can be an attractive addition to your garden.

When birds bathe, particularly in large numbers at a time, they can get quite excited and energetic, splashing water all about. Unless you want a soggy, muddy area around the bath, set it on a pad that will quickly absorb or drain off water. Gravel or sand works best. For a 30-inch birdbath, remove about 4 inches of soil from an area about 4 feet square, and refill the depression with gravel. Set the birdbath in place so that it is level. Dark-colored river gravel, pea gravel, or sand is attractive, but there are many decorative gravels from which to choose.

Small Easy Pools

A small pool useful to birds can be nothing more than a birdbath set into the ground. Some simple pools can even be large enough for a few fish and water plants.

The easiest kind of small pool to provide is the basin of a birdbath; heavy concrete ones work best. Dig a depression deep enough so that the lip of the basin will extend up from the ground level about 2 inches to prevent soil from washing in. Set the basin in place, backfill around the edges, and you have a small garden pool in a matter of minutes.

Another easy way to build a small garden pool is to dig out the soil to any depth and shape you wish, using some of the soil you dig up to build a small mound about 6 inches higher than ground level and about 12 inches wide all the way around the edge. Tamp the soil in the depression and the mounded edge until it is well compacted. While you are tamping, create a

Easy Birdbaths to Make

Garbage can lid

Tile drainage pipe

Ceramic saucer on tree stump

Rock for weight

Naturally formed river rock

Chiselled stump or log

small trench in the mound around the hole about 4 inches deep and 6 inches back from the edge. Then line the hole with a heavy sheet of polyethylene, plastic, or rubber, allowing its edges to extend outside the perimeter by about a foot. Fold the excess down into the trench, and cover it with gravel. You are ready to fill your pool with water. Black or dark brown plastic is more attractive and less noticeable than a lighter color. You can hide it by scattering gravel on the bottom of the pool and lining the sides and top of the edges with small flat rocks set carefully in place so they don't tear the plastic. This also helps to hold the lining in place.

A bit more expensive, but also more permanent, is to use one of the ready-made pools formed out of fiberglass or plastic, available at garden centers and hardware stores. Simply dig out soil to fit the shape of the pool (usually round or kidney-shaped), set it in place, backfill where necessary, and fill it with water.

Wine and vinegar kegs, and old bathtubs, can receive the same treatment for interesting garden pools. You don't even have to bury them in the ground, as long as you drain them before freezing weather sets in. When used above ground, these items have the advantage of easy drainage for cleaning. In any pool that doesn't have gradually sloping sides, or that is deeper than a few inches, you will have to provide a place for birds to alight, as described on page 50.

Musical, Moving Water

The sound of gently moving water is extremely appealing to birds. In fact, bird banders often lure them with dripping water. Audible water in the garden can be provided by a simple dripping hose or by a sophisticated waterfall that requires complex plumbing. However you supply it, remember that a little water music goes a long way. A thunderous waterfall or a huge erupting fountain will frighten more birds than it attracts. Small drips, tinkles, and burbles are what birds like.

The easiest way to provide water music is to suspend a bucket from a tree limb 4 or 5 feet above the basin of a birdbath. Punch a small hole with a nail in the side of the bucket about 1/2 inch from the bottom; even the smallest particles of debris will clog up the tiny hole if it is in the

Easy Garden Pools

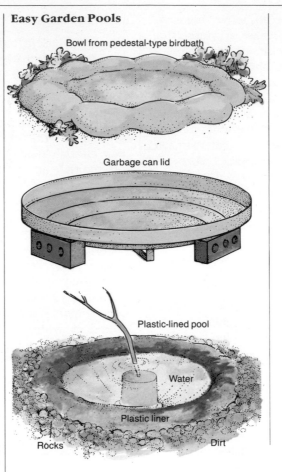

Bowl from pedestal-type birdbath

Garbage can lid

Plastic-lined pool

Water

Plastic liner

Rocks   Dirt

A Simple Waterfall

A series of basins dug into a sloping hillside, with a pump to recirculate the water, makes a simple attractive waterfall.

bottom. Cover the top of the bucket to keep out as much debris as possible. Start with a very small hole. Ten or twenty drops per minute are plenty; you can always make the hole larger if necessary.

A more attractive alternative is to run a small-diameter clear plastic tube up the trunk of a tree and out a low-hanging branch over the birdbath. An adapter will enable you to connect the tubing to the garden hose and disconnect it easily when you need the hose for other purposes. A shut-off clamp with an adjustable screw attached to the outflow end of the tube will allow precise regulation of the water flow.

Many birds love to fly through mist and fine sprays. Hang a hose with the nozzle set on mist spray over a tree branch or some other raised support. Or use the kind of soaker hose that emits mist or fine streams of water. Turn the water on at regular times of the day, and birds will quickly learn when to expect this treat. Hummingbirds are very fond of bathing this way.

Fountains and waterfalls in the garden are as pleasing to people as they are to birds. Some birdbaths are equipped with fountains and jet sprays that bubble or

spray up from the center of the pool. A simple waterfall can be constructed as a series of basins, with water falling from one to another. Whether you buy a kit or purchase the necessary hardware separately, be sure that the basin is deep enough to keep the pump out of sight and covered with water.

Natural-looking waterfalls and streams require great artistry and technical expertise to build. They can add an exciting dimension to your garden, however, and many people consider hiring a professional landscape architect for this job well worth the expense. Remember, though, that shallow areas and a gentle flow of water are the keys to attracting birds.

If you want to build a waterfall yourself, keep it small and simple. An easy one is based on the same principle as the birdbath dug into the ground. On a sloping hillside, dig in a series of such basins so that they overlap, one above the other, in stairstep fashion. Pay special attention to the angle and sharpness of each lip over which the water will flow. The idea is to prevent water from flowing or dripping back up under the basin, loosening soil and washing it into the system. The lip should be sharp and at a slight downward tilt so that water falls cleanly over the edge.

The bottom pool, or an adjacent hidden chamber, should be deep enough to hold the pump. Clear flexible plastic tubing will return this water from the bottom basin back to the top, and can be hidden from view by burying it in the ground or growing plants over it. The size of the pump you need will be determined by the intended rate of flow (which should be slow for the birds' sake) and by how much higher the top basin is than the lowest one.

Consider carefully the placement of any birdbath, fountain, pool, or waterfall that requires electricity. It's not wise to use extension cords as permanent garden fixtures. In many areas their use is prohibited by local law. Since your fountain, birdbath, or pool is a permanent garden fixture, consider hiring an electrician to run a line out to it, with a switch inside the house. The safety and convenience are well worth the effort. Such a line can double for the water heater you might use in winter, or for attractive lighting at night.

Moving Water in the Garden

Dripping, splashing, musical water is particularly appealing to birds.

Dripping hose

Bucket with hole

Birdbath fountain

PROVIDING NESTING SITES

Birdhouses of specific shapes and dimensions attract specific birds. In this chapter you'll find a plan for a basic birdhouse to build, with variations for different birds.

What a quiet, sad season spring would be without the music of birds. Proclaiming their territory and courting their mates, many of our favorite garden birds announce the start of their busiest season. Their elaborate territory stakeouts and courtship rituals are only the beginning. Selecting a nesting site, collecting nesting materials and building a nest (which can take thousands of trips over a week or more), laying eggs and patiently incubating them, nurturing, feeding, warming, and protecting the helpless nestlings that emerge, and leading the infants to maturity—all arc jobs that will completely occupy the busy parents for the summer months.

Attracting Breeding Pairs

Many factors are important in a bird's choice of a nesting site, and most of them are beyond our control. We can do much, however, to encourage birds to nest in our yards. The most important thing to remember is: be patient. Birds may take awhile—several seasons, even—to discover our efforts.

Some birds are especially territorial during the breeding season. The size of a breeding territory varies with the species, from many square miles for some birds of prey, to less than an acre for the American Robin and Red-winged Blackbird. For some birds that nest in communities, like Purple Martins, the "territory," if it can be called that, may be only a few inches. The size of a territory can fluctuate from individual to individual within a species, depending on competition, population level, and available food and nesting sites. Some birds, like mockingbirds, defend their territories with extraordinary zeal, attacking intruding birds and other creatures (including humans) much larger than themselves.

Unless you live on property of estate dimensions, it is unlikely you will attract more than one pair of a territorial species; each pair will drive away all competing individuals of their own kind. Of course, your land may straddle a territorial boundary, and feeders may attract several such adjacent pairs. However, because they prefer different feeding and nesting sites, different species can and often do nest in surprisingly close neighborliness, and it is quite possible to have a number of nesting pairs of different kinds of birds raising their young in the same small yard.

In order to increase the number of breeding pairs in your garden, then, we recommend the approach mentioned throughout this book: diversity. The greater the number of types of plants, birdhouses, and nesting materials you provide, the greater the variety of nesting birds that will be drawn to your garden. Ten birdhouses of the same style and dimensions in one garden may draw only a single pair of birds, while the other nine remain empty.

This chapter describes the kinds of shelter you can provide for birds in your garden. For specific information on the nesting habits of the birds most likely to take advantage of your hospitality, see the "Gallery of Birds," beginning on page 65.

The American Robin may raise two or three broods each year. Left, sitting on the nest. Right, gathering nesting materials.

Nesting Materials

The provision of suitable nesting materials can be a powerful inducement for birds to nest in your garden. A single nest often consists of a thousand or even several thousand pieces, each requiring an individual search-and-carry mission. Particularly in super-clean gardens where every dead twig is pruned off and thrown away, where every mown blade of grass or loose leaf is swept up into plastic bags, the availability of nesting materials can be a strongly limiting factor in choice of a nest site.

When a human being provides nesting materials, they can be offered in concentrated, readily-observable piles and stashes, reducing the time it takes a bird to find things and build a nest. Even if all you offer is a bundle of dead twigs, concentrating them in one spot can be of significant value to birds. Empty suet feeders and wire baskets hung from a branch or nailed to a tree are both excellent places to offer nesting materials; they are convenient for the birds, and the wind can't scatter the pieces. If you offer nesting materials loose, be sure to place them in a conspicuous spot out in the open, such as on the lawn or draped over a clothesline.

It's a good idea to cut stringy materials into lengths no longer than 8 inches, as longer pieces of string, yarn, and such things have been reported to cause entanglement and even strangulation when looped and woven into a nest. Don't place materials directly in a birdhouse, as it will look as though it is already occupied. Remember, of course, that any of these man-made items that aren't used by birds become litter if not kept in a restricted area. See the illustration for some suggested ways to present nesting materials.

Several birds, including American Robins, Wood Thrushes, Eastern Phoebes, and Barn and Cliff Swallows, require mud to construct their nests. You can assist and encourage their nearby nesting if you keep a supply handy during the nest-building season. Not too much is necessary—a garbage can lid sunk into an out-of-the-way corner, kept full of wet, sticky clay soil, is plenty.

Above left: Finding and collecting nesting materials is a major task for breeding birds, requiring hundreds or even thousands of trips. This female Eastern Bluebird has quite a mouthful. Above: Some birds, like the Cliff Swallow, require a convenient source of mud for nest construction.

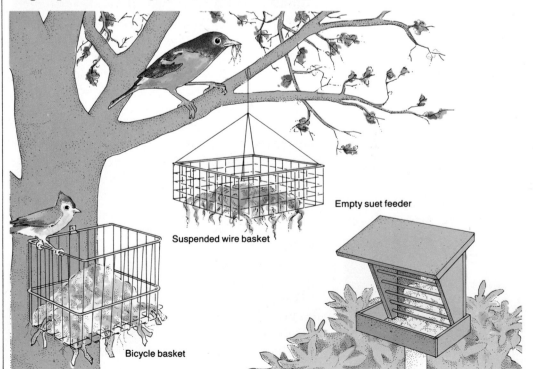

Empty suet feeder

Suspended wire basket

Bicycle basket

Some Ways to Present Nesting Materials

Materials useful to birds for building nests include stringy materials like yarn, string, and narrow strips of soft cloth, and fuzzy materials like shredded absorbent cotton, hair combed from pets, excelsior, feathers, and stuffing from old furniture.

Birdhouses

About fifty species of North American birds are known to use birdhouses for nesting. The ones most likely to nest in the garden are given in the chart on page 94. Except for House Finches and House Sparrows, most of these birds naturally nest in cavities or crevices, rather than constructing nests on tree limbs, in shrubs, or on the ground. The widespread practice of "clean" forestry, agriculture, and gardening has severely reduced the available nesting sites in old, decaying trees in many areas. We can assist birds by supplying "cavities" in the form of birdhouses, or nesting boxes. A wide variety of commercially made birdhouses are available for purchase from hardware stores, garden centers, and mail-order firms advertised in such magazines as *Audubon*. Some are ready-made, others come in easy-to-assemble kits. Or you can make your own—an easy, inexpensive, and interesting hobby.

Above: *Don't limit your imagination in constructing a birdhouse. A milk carton, protected by an additional roof, makes an excellent short-term nesting box for this Tree Swallow. Since milk cartons are impervious to moisture and "breathing," punch several holes for ventilation and drainage. And because milk cartons overheat in direct sunlight, place them in shady locations.*

Left: *Breeding birds feed their young huge quantities of insects. The Eastern Bluebird eats mostly insects the year round, although its consumption of fruit increases in the late summer. Even most confirmed seedeaters switch to insects while they are raising their young.* Bottom: *In areas, and years, in which House Wrens are highly populous, they may pierce the eggs of other bird species in their breeding territory.*

The Basic Birdhouse

The illustrations accompanying this section present design and construction plans for you to build your own birdhouse. This design is adaptable to nearly all cavity-nesting birds; consult the chart on page 94 for the dimensions appropriate to the species of bird you wish to attract. In building or buying a birdhouse, keep the following points in mind:

o A birdhouse should be designed and built for a particular species. Nesting boxes said to appeal to a wide variety will probably appeal to none—or to the wrong ones. When purchasing a birdhouse, always ask for one by the bird's name—a House Wren box, or a Northern Flicker house. Style and construction of birdhouses can be very similar; the important difference between species is in the dimensions. The diameter and placement of the entrance hole, and the depth, width, and height of the interior (including available floor space) are the important dimensions to know. Nevertheless, many species are close enough in their favored dimensions that the bird you get may not be the one you expected.

o Except for Purple Martin houses, a birdhouse should be designed for a single nest. "Duplexes" and "triplexes" are a waste of effort and materials, as a bird's territorial tendencies will prevent occupancy of more than one cavity.

o Generally the simplest, plainest design, painted or stained with a subdued color, will be the most attractive to birds. Many commercially built birdhouses, and designs for building your own, are loaded with useless doodads and frills. Such cute birdhouses are designed more for garden decoration than for attracting birds. Especially avoid birdhouses with parts that move in the wind, or that are made of highly reflective materials.

o Materials for birdhouse construction should be weather-resistant and durable, so that they last several years, stay dry inside, and "breathe" well with no moisture buildup. Birdhouses should be well insulated to remain warm on cool days and cool on hot days. The latter is especially important, as many birds prefer their houses to be placed in open, sunny spots. About the only material

Some Commercially Available Birdhouses

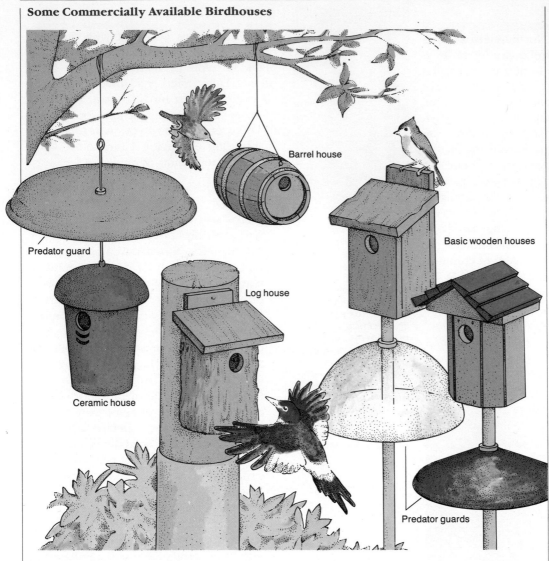

Predator guard

Barrel house

Basic wooden houses

Ceramic house

Log house

Predator guards

Opposite page: *Construction plans for basic birdhouse.*

The roof of the birdhouse should carry away water. It needs to be sloping, and should overlap the front and sides by at least 1½ inches. It is best not to hinge the roof for opening and cleaning, as the hinge is difficult to seal against the rain. Hinge one of the sides instead. One inch back from the front edge of the roof, score a drip line ⅛ inch deep on the underside, to keep water from running into the seams and entrance.

Do not attach a perch on the outside by the entrance. Birds don't need it, and it will only help squirrels and cats to raid the nest. However, on the inside, just below the entrance hole, attach one or two small, horizontal cleats to assist the parents and the young in their exit. A series of horizontal cuts ⅛ inch deep will serve the same purpose.

Good ventilation is essential to prevent heat buildup. At the top of each side, drill three ¼-inch holes for ventilation. The ventilation holes should always be drilled above the level of the entrance hole to avoid drafts.

One side of the birdhouse should be removable or hinged to permit removal of old nests and cleaning after the nestlings have left. However, the opening side must be able to be locked firmly in place while the box is in use.

The bottom should have good drainage in case water gets into the box during a storm. Unless drainage is otherwise provided for, drill three ¼-inch holes into the bottom of the box.

that meets these standards is wood 3/4 inch or 1 inch thick, with galvanized steel or brass hardware (nails, screws, hinges, and clasps). Among the woods that are the most durable and easiest to work with are redwood, white cedar, and cypress. Lumber should be well seasoned, since green or wet wood will warp and split. Avoid houses made of metal, which may bake the baby birds, and of plastic, because moisture will build up inside. Exceptions are commercially made aluminum houses for Purple Martins, which are designed for good air circulation (see page 62).

o Each section of the birdhouse should be treated with a wood preservative before assembly. Paint is somewhat less satisfactory, but better than nothing. Natural, dull colors, especially browns, grays, and greens, are best for attracting birds. White can be useful to keep tempera-

tures down in the hot sun, and many species of birds don't seem to mind it.

o The birdhouse mounting should be strong, secure, and stable. Loosely mounted boxes that can jiggle or sway in the wind or when a parent alights are not attractive to birds (except for wrens, which accept hanging houses) and court possible disaster. If even the slightest chance exists of a birdhouse coming loose and falling to the ground, it is a potential deathtrap. The two most common ways of mounting a birdhouse are on top of a post or sturdy pole, or nailed (or preferably screwed) to a vertical support like a tree. Overlapping the back piece by at least 2 inches on the sides or bottom provides a convenient place to nail up the nesting box. Obviously, it is important to know where and how you plan on securing the bird box before buying or building it.

o Weather protection is also important in mounting the birdhouse. The entrance hole should be directed away from the path of prevailing winds; in most places this means facing south or southeast. Do not mount a birdhouse so that the entrance side faces up even slightly, as it will collect rain. A slight downward tilt is best. When nailing or screwing a birdhouse to a wall, post, or tree, insert a small strip of wood on either side of the back, so that there is a space between the back and what it is mounted against. This will prevent water from collecting and soaking through the back piece.

Some birds prefer a nesting shelf to an enclosed box. See below and right for construction details.

Nesting Shelves

American Robins, Eastern Phoebes, and Barn Swallows can sometimes be persuaded to use nesting shelves (see illustration on this page, and dimensions in the chart on page 94). Essentially, these nesting shelves are birdhouses without sides or front. They should be mounted under overhanging eaves against the house, garage, or garden shed. In the case of American Robins, a vine-covered arbor is an especially attractive location.

The Barn Swallow shelf is designed somewhat differently from the others, without a roof, and should definitely have the protection of an overhanging eave. Barn and Cliff Swallows nest together in communities. Both species can be encouraged to nest on the side of a building by attaching 2×4s horizontally against a wall and providing an adequate supply of mud out in the open for them to use in building nests.

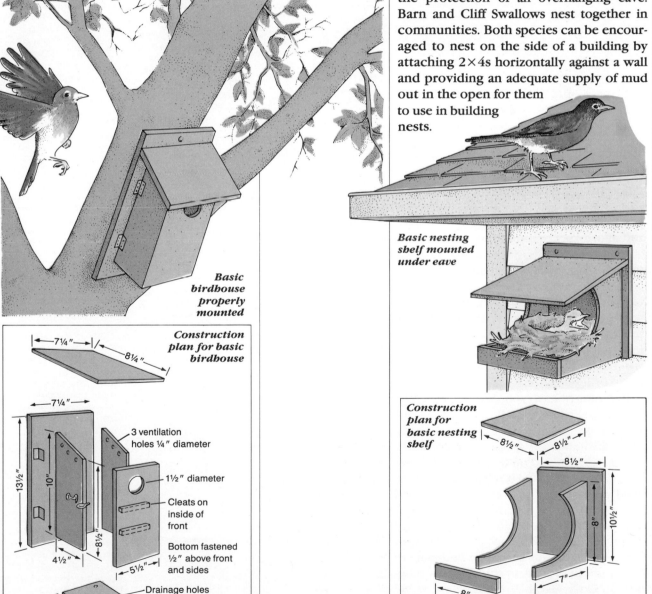

Basic birdhouse properly mounted

Basic nesting shelf mounted under eave

Construction plan for basic birdhouse

7¼″ 8¼″

7¼″

3 ventilation holes ¼″ diameter

1½″ diameter

Cleats on inside of front

Bottom fastened ½″ above front and sides

Drainage holes

13½″   10″   8½″

4½″   5½″

4½″   4½″

Construction plan for basic nesting shelf

8½″   8½″

8½″

10½″   8″

8″   7″   7″   7″

Placement of Birdhouses

It is usually a waste of effort to erect more than one birdhouse attractive to a particular species of bird in a garden of less than one acre. There are a few exceptions to this rule, however. Tree Swallows will accept fairly close neighbors of their own kind. Nesting boxes intended for them can be as close together as 30 feet. The boxes should be mounted on posts, well out in the open, and near or standing in water. Wrens, although territorial, like to have a considerable choice of nesting sites. The male House Wren arrives early in the spring, before the female, and constructs as many as a dozen nests in his territory. He then courts a female by taking her around and showing off his work. When she finally accepts one of his nesting sites, a mating bond is formed. As often as not, the first thing she does is tear apart his hard work and start all over. Because of this ritual, setting out four or more wren boxes is a powerful attraction for one pair of these delightful birds.

Some boxes built to specific dimensions for a certain bird may be used by birds of a different species if they are of the same size or smaller. In this case providing several identical birdhouses is an advantage, and another exception to the rule.

It is difficult to say how many different types of birdhouses will be occupied in one area, because there are too many variations between gardens, habitats, and year-to-year population changes. Sizes of territories fluctuate as well. About ten different types of birdhouses per acre is a good start, but some gardens may support more or less than that.

It is best to have your birdhouses up by late summer or early fall, while the leaves are still on the trees. The extent of shadiness, an important factor to many birds, can be determined better before the trees lose their leaves. And birdhouses that have aged and weathered over the winter will be more attractive to birds.

If you are unable to get your birdhouses up in the early fall, you should plan on mounting them no later than mid-January in the mildest parts of the country, or as late as early March in the coldest. Some birds start nesting later. The Northern Flicker, for example, usually starts building a nest around the middle of May.

A Special House for Purple Martins

The interesting social behavior of Purple Martins, along with their rich song, graceful flight, and the consumption of tens of thousands of mosquitoes and other flying insects, makes it well worth the effort to attract them with suitable housing.

Formerly, the only way you could have a Purple Martin house was to build one yourself—a complicated project that frequently resulted in heavy structures difficult to raise or lower, and inconvenient to take apart and maintain. If you are a confirmed do-it-yourselfer, and have the experience and equipment to do the job, you may enjoy building one yourself. The best plan for a martin house is available from the Superintendent of Documents, U.S. Government Printing Office, Washington, D.C. 20402. Send $2.50 and ask for "Homes for Birds," Conservation Bulletin #14, Stock #024-010-00524-4.

In most cases metal nesting boxes are not recommended for birds. The only exception is for Purple Martins. Extensive testing has resulted in houses designed for good air circulation and exceptional heat-reflecting capacity—two very important criteria to look for. Commercially made aluminum martin houses have several advantages over homemade wooden ones. They are light, easy to put up and take down, and more weather-resistant, requiring less refinishing maintenance. Whether you buy or build your own, your martin house should meet the following requirements:

o Each nesting compartment of the martin house should be built to the correct dimensions (see the chart on page 94).

o The best martin houses are expandable, so that you can add new floors and compartments as the colony grows from year to year. Houses have been built with over a hundred compartments, but it is best to start small, with eight to twelve.

o It should be correctly placed. If you don't have a suitable location for a martin house, there is little chance it will be used. A martin house should be mounted on a pole 12 to 20 feet high in an open lawn or meadow at least 40 feet from any nearby tree, structure, or other flight obstruction. Even shrubs or small trees over 5 feet tall near the martin house are a hindrance to these birds, as they like to approach the nest in long gliding swoops. Nearby bodies of water and large, open lawns and meadows are a

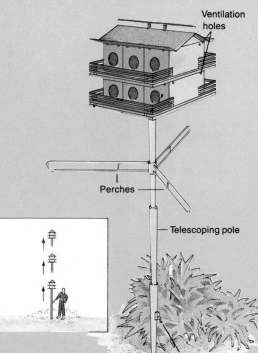

Ventilation holes

Perches

Telescoping pole

Crank

Purple Martin Apartment House

This commercially available martin house is made of light-weight aluminum and features a telescoping pole that can be cranked up and down to make cleaning easy.

Opposite page, above: *This home-made Martin house provides good ventilation for each compartment, as well as a means to clean each compartment individually.* Below: *Hanging gourds make imaginative and attractive houses for Purple Martins.*

distinct plus, as martins hunt insects on the wing and need large areas without flight obstructions to do so. Telephone or utility wires about 30 yards from the martin house are another advantage, providing them with a perch.

o The martin house should have good ventilation either from holes cut into each compartment above the entrance, a central air shaft that allows rising heat to escape through attic vents, or both.

o The martin house should be easily raised and lowered. It will need to be taken down yearly and cleaned out before the martins return in spring. Wooden houses should be stored under cover in winter. Many aluminum houses feature a convenient pulley-and-winch apparatus or telescoping pole.

Maintaining the Birdhouse

An important part of attracting birds with nesting boxes is maintenance. For birds that are likely to start more than one brood per season, the nesting box should be cleaned out as soon as the young have fledged. This is particularly important because parasites are a major cause of nestling mortality. Most birds will seldom use a nest a second time; boxes containing dirty old nests will be abandoned in favor of a new spot. If you clean out the box right away, they may decide to use it again; in any case, it will be ready for another pair looking for a place to raise a second brood.

Open the removable side and clean out the old nest and any debris that has collected. It is a good idea to fumigate, spray, or dust the box to destroy any parasites it might be harboring. This task should be done each time a pair has completed raising a brood.

If you open the box and there are signs that the brood was unsuccessful (unhatched eggs, dead infants), don't touch anything, and close the box back up again, as the parents are likely to start a second attempt immediately. If so, they will do the cleanup themselves.

Once the birdhouse is occupied, do not disturb it or move it for any reason. Some people remark on the fearlessness and "tameness" of incubating parents. The fact is that there are few better ways to make a bird abandon its young for good than to open the box and look in on them. If you simply cannot restrain yourself from peeking in on the nestlings, be absolutely certain the parents are not around. Do not open the box; a loosely made nest may fall to the ground. It is best if you learn to enjoy the activity from afar.

Discouraging Starlings and House Sparrows

Entrance holes 1-1/2 inches or less in diameter will exclude starlings, but they need to be 1-1/8 inches or less to exclude House Sparrows. Unfortunately, this size entrance hole also excludes many desirable birds. Another possible approach is to mount birdhouses just as the desired species is returning in the spring. This is effective only with birds that are faithful to the same nesting spot year after year, like Purple Martins, and requires close observation and readiness on your part.

Protection from Predators

Birdhouses should be placed where cats and squirrels can't reach them. Because of the threat of such predators, birds are cautious about choosing a nesting box on the main trunk of a tree. If you do put a birdhouse in such a place, cats can be discouraged by wrapping a smooth metal collar around the trunk that is at least 18 inches deep and 5 feet up from the ground. Make sure that the seams don't provide a toehold. You must check this collar at least twice a year; if it is not frequently adjusted, it will girdle and kill a growing tree. Protecting a post or a pole from climbing intruders is much easier, and most people prefer to mount their birdhouses in this way. If you use a wooden post, use the cone-shaped squirrel guard recommended for bird feeders.

A post- or pole-mounted bird house is also superior because, generally speaking, birds prefer an open, sunny spot to dense shade for their nesting boxes. Near the edge of a woods, facing south over an open expanse, is an excellent location for many birds, as are open, grassy areas with a few trees, like abandoned orchards. There are exceptions, of course, including the deep-woods dwellers like some woodpeckers, nuthatches, and chickadees.

Whether the birdhouse or shelf is placed in a tree, on a post, or under an eave or arbor, it should have a clear, unobstructed flight path to the entrance hole. A perch from 5 to 15 feet away from the nesting box will be used to survey for danger before the final approach, and will serve as a resting spot for the "off-duty" parent.

Cellophane is an attractive nesting material for many birds, as in this Gray Catbird nest.

GALLERY OF BIRDS

Here's information about the habitat, range, food, and nesting preferences of 75 species of birds that are likely to visit your garden.

Considering how specialized birds are, the number of species that frequent our gardens is truly remarkable. This guide discusses many of the outstanding bird species that often show up around the home. Each entry includes a photograph, a brief description of the bird, and a range map that shows whether or not a species inhabits your part of the country. You will also find specific information about the habitat, feeding, and nesting requirements of each bird in the wild, and how to fill those needs in the garden.

If you follow our recommendations for increasing the attractiveness of your garden to the birds included in this guide, you are likely to receive visits by less common birds as well. The sight of a rare bird at the windowsill is a thrill to remember. You may want to purchase one of the many excellent field guides to birds, not only to identify the rare visitor, but to more positively identify the ones you see every day. The photographs and short descriptions in this guide will start you on the way, but are not intended to substitute for a field guide. In many cases the brief descriptions and photographs are of adult male birds in breeding plumage. Females, juveniles, and males in nonbreeding plumage look quite different, and some species are differentiated from closely related ones by traits too subtle to treat here in depth.

The sequence in which we have presented birds in this guide deserves some comment. The grouping of birds into families, and then species within those families, is the standard method

used by all authoritative field guides and other references on birds. Families, in turn, are grouped within orders, and the whole list reflects the sequence of evolutionary development as it is presently understood by ornithologists. The authority for all such reference books is the American Ornithologists' Union Check-list of North American Birds, which is periodically updated to reflect new information on the evolutionary origins of birds. The most current revision of the Check-list was completed in July of 1982, and is the one we use here. This sequence not only makes this book more easily used with other references on birds, such as field guides, but also gives valuable information about the relationships between bird species. The fact that birds are limited to breeding within a group of very similar members makes possible the striking differences between species, and the uniformity within species, that we use for identification. Be sure that any field guide you purchase uses this 1982 revised check-list.

If you prefer an alphabetical listing, use the index at the back of this book; boldface type tells you where that bird species is found in the "Gallery of Birds" for quick, easy reference.

How to Use the Range Map

The range maps that accompany each entry are based on information provided by the *Audubon Society Field Guides to North American Birds.* In these maps the breeding range is shown in beige, the winter range in blue, and the permanent range in green. For a discussion of the ranges, and of the seasonal movements of birds between their ranges, see page 14.

Formerly known as the Baltimore Oriole, this bird has recently been lumped with the Bullock's Oriole of the western United States into a single species, now called the Northern Oriole.

American Kestrel

Northern Bobwhite

California Quail

American Kestrel
(Falcon Family)

Because it occasionally eats small songbirds, this falcon—formerly called Sparrow Hawk—frequently meets a mixed reception in the bird garden. It performs a valuable service to the bird community, however, in weeding out weak and slower individuals. The majority of its diet is insects. This jay-sized bird has long, pointed wings and a rusty tail and back. The wings of the male are pale blue-gray; those of the female are rusty. In prey and habitat requirements it is the daytime counterpart of the nocturnal Screech Owl.

Habitat: The American Kestrel prefers open country, especially parks, farmlands, and plains studded with a few trees or giant cacti, or adjacent to woodland and wooded canyons.

It frequently resides in open areas at the edges of cities, towns, and suburbs, highways and utility right-of-ways, and sometimes even in urban areas. A garden may attract a nesting pair if it resembles a woodland edge, or borders on open pastures, fields, parkland, or prairie. Nesting territory averages about 250 acres per pair, but may be less or more depending on population pressure and food availability.
Nesting: The American Kestrel does not build a nest, but lays eggs in the cavities of tall trees or cacti, on the ledges of cliffs, in holes of buildings (especially under eaves and gables), and in nesting boxes. It prefers abandoned flicker holes, and sometimes competes with this bird, Screech Owls, and squirrels for nesting cavities. This is the only North American falcon that will readily nest in a bird box, which should be placed in a tree or tall cactus next to an open area, from 10 to 30 feet above the ground. The breeding season starts in early March in Florida;

mid-April in the central United States; and late May in southern Canada.
Feeding: The American Kestrel feeds primarily on large insects (mainly grasshoppers) and small rodents, but occasionally eats small songbirds. In populated areas, the prolific House Sparrow is among its favorite prey. In arid climates it is able to extract all the water it needs from its food.

Northern Bobwhite
(Pheasant Family)

These ground-dwelling quail often surprise the hiker in brushy fields with a loud explosion of wings, as a covey scatters in every direction. They are speedy on foot or on wing for short distances. They spend a large part of every day resting, and are especially fond of daily bathing. The Bobwhite is a plump red-brown bird. The male has a white throat and a white stripe over the eyes. In the female these markings are buff-colored.

Habitat: These birds live in forest edges, brushy old fields and pastures, farmlands, wild roadside hedges, brushy fence rows,

grasslands with nearby wooded river valleys, canyons, ravines, or scattered trees and shrubs. They are frequent visitors to rural and suburban parks if provided with a dense cover of shrubs and low trees near open lawns, flower beds, and herbaceous borders.
Nesting: The Northern Bobwhite lays eggs in a shallow scrape in the ground lined with grasses and leaves, concealed by arched grasses and weeds, in open grasslands or near hedges and brushy fence-rows, thickets, and brush-piles. It also nests in hay, grain, and alfalfa fields, and roosts in coveys at night on the ground in brushy fields and grasslands.
Feeding: These birds feed on the ground, and seldom fly unless forced to. They may forage over wide areas, and wander restlessly, especially in the fall of the year. They travel and feed in pairs, small families, or coveys of up to 15 individuals. About 70 percent of their diet is vegetable; the rest is insects. They eat the seeds and fruits of grasses; many legumes, including soybeans, bush clover, cowpeas, and peanuts; partridgeberries, pine seeds, acorns, seeds of sweet gum, maples, ashes and beeches, sassafras and sumac. They enjoy most fruits and berries. Northern Bobwhites often come to feeding stations in the winter, where they pick

up food from the ground. Favorite winter foods include millet, cracked corn, buckwheat, wheat, and sunflower seeds. The Northern Bobwhite is a shy bird, easily frightened away by loud noises. It has been known to chase starlings from feeders. It is regular in its habits, feeding for an hour or so in early mid-morning, and again in late afternoon, storing large amounts of food in its crop for later digestion. The rest of the day is spent resting.

California Quail
(Pheasant Family)

This quail, the western counterpart of the eastern Bobwhite, is a common dooryard and garden bird throughout much of the far West. This plump gray bird has a black plume that tilts forward from the top of the dark brown head. A speedy runner that resorts to flight only when it absolutely must, it nevertheless flies very fast for short distances. During the breeding season, the male and female and their chicks are seen together. In the winter, families combine into coveys of up to 60 individuals, with a rigid social structure and behavior system. Prolific breeders, they

Rock Dove

Mourning Dove

have been hunted heavily for market and sport. They are nonmigratory.

Habitat: These birds reside where low trees and shrubs are broken in patches by low grasses and herbaceous plants, nearly always close to a source of water like a stream, pool, or irrigation ditch. In the garden, a combination of dense shrubby cover and mixed herbaceous borders is especially inviting, and a source of drinking water on the ground will be popular. California Quail roost at night in low tree branches 15 to 25 feet off the ground.

Nesting: The nest is usually a shallow scrape in the ground, lined with grass, in a clump of tall grasses and weeds, under a shrub or brushpile, or out in the open next to a rock or log. California Quail have been known to build nests up to 10 feet off the ground in the fork of a tree branch or in a vine. They readily nest in gardens, often right next to frequently used paths near the house. Dense flower beds and borders, shrubs and hedges, and clumps of cacti are favorite garden nesting spots. These prolific quail breed from January to October in California, and from May to July farther north where winters are severe.

Feeding: California Quail are very habitual in their feeding; they return again and again to the same feeding ground if food is abundant. They feed an hour or so every morning just after dawn, and an hour or so every evening just before sunset. The rest of the day they rest, or congregate around drinking places. They eat primarily vegetable matter, but occasionally consume insects. They feed almost entirely on the ground, or just off the ground in the low branches of shrubs. Favorite foods include the seeds of clover, lupine, and vetch, all kinds of grain, grasses, acorns, berries, and grapes. Bush clover is a favorite food shrub.

Rock Dove
(Pigeon Family)

This familiar bird was introduced to the United States in the early 1600s. Raised in captivity since ancient times, it has become established in most cities of the world. Known to many as the "common pigeon" and "carrier pigeon" of cities, parks, and home dovecotes, it is one of the few birds to visit deep urban window feeders. Most commonly gray or gray and white with iridescent neck feathers, this bird comes in a seemingly endless variety of patterns. Because it has been accused of transmitting several human diseases, many consider it a pest and have futilely attempted its eradication.

Habitat: The original preferred habitats of Rock Doves were high cliffs, ledges, and caves near the sea. They have adapted to the "urban cliffs" of tall city buildings, and are common in city and suburban parks and gardens, as well as farmlands.

Nesting: Rock Doves build a loose platform nest of twigs and grasses on the ledges of buildings, under bridges, on beams and rafters in barns and other farm outbuildings, and sometimes on flat roofs, eaves, and under the rain gutters of suburban homes. Many people are more concerned with discouraging Rock Doves from nesting than with encouraging them. Flashings placed at a 45-degree angle on favorite nesting spots on ledges, flat roofs, and gutters can help.

Feeding: Rock Doves feed on the ground, usually in flocks numbering from a few to several hundred individuals. In cities, they readily learn to accept hand feeding. They are frequent visitors to the garden feeder in urban and suburban areas, eating from ground feeders and on the ground beneath raised feeders. Their favorite foods include grain of all kinds, especially corn, wheat, and buckwheat. White millet, bakery goods, and table scraps are also popular.

Mourning Dove
(Pigeon Family)

In winter the Mourning Dove is a gregarious bird, traveling in flocks of up to 20 individuals. A soft gray-brown with a tapered white-edged tail, this bird is a regular visitor to many winter feeding stations.

Habitat: The Mourning Dove prefers open land with scattered trees and shrubs. It is one of the most widespread and adaptable North American birds, however, and thrives in habitats as diverse as eastern woodlands, midwestern open plains, and western mesquite deserts and scrub, in altitudes ranging from sea level to 13,000-foot mountain slopes. It frequently visits streams, pools, and other drinking and bathing spots. The best garden habitat for Mourning Doves includes open lawn, herbaceous borders, and flower beds, with scattered patches of trees and shrubs, and a source of water on the ground. They often appear in urban and suburban gardens, particularly those close to open fields.

Nesting: Mourning Doves frequently nest in gardens, especially if food and water are convenient and abundant. The nest is a loose platform constructed 5 to 25 feet above the ground, often in the crotch of a shrub or tree. Other supports are also commonly used, including vines, gutters and chimneys of houses, and the nests of other birds. Mourning Doves breed April through August in their northern range; February through September in the South; and virtually any season in California.

Feeding: Mourning Doves subsist mostly on seeds picked up from the ground. Favorite foods in the wild include waste grain, especially corn and wheat, and many grass and weed seeds. Sweet gum, alder, hollies, elders, spruces, and serviceberries are favorite garden plants for food. These birds are frequent visitors to bird feeders in winter, where they prefer to eat at ground feeders and on the ground under raised feeders. White and red proso millet, oil-type sunflower seeds, and canary seed are their favorite foods, along with black-striped and hulled sunflower seeds, milo, corn, buckwheat, and wheat.

Screech Owl

Chimney Swift

Ruby-throated Hummingbird

Screech Owl
(Owl Family)

These small owls rest quietly during the day in cavities or on branches close to the trunks of densely foliaged trees. They become active and hunt at night. East of the Rockies they may be brown, rust-brown, or gray. In the western United States they are usually gray. In prey, nesting sites, and habitat, the Screech Owl is the nighttime counterpart of the American Kestrel. They often nest around gardens.

Habitat: The Screech Owl prefers open woods, woodland edges bordering open fields, old fields with scattered trees and shrubs, and, in the Southwest, deserts with giant saguaro cacti, wooded canyons, and wooded streams and lakeshores. An occasional visitor and resident of rural and suburban yards and gardens, the Screech

Owl prefers gardens with many trees and adjoining open areas for hunting. It drinks and bathes frequently, and appreciates a source of water for its nocturnal visits.

Nesting: The Screech Owl lays its eggs in the cavities of trees, stumps, and saguaro cacti, sometimes in natural holes but often in abandoned flicker holes. It generally uses no nesting materials. It will nest in a bird box built to the appropriate dimensions and mounted in a tree 10 to 30 feet above the ground. Screech Owls compete with the flickers, American Kestrels, and squirrels for nesting sites. They breed from February to July in southern regions, and for a shorter period in spring and early summer in the North. Nesting boxes are also useful as roosting boxes in winter.

Feeding: Screech Owls are strictly nocturnal hunters, subsisting chiefly on large insects, small rodents, and, more rarely, small reptiles and songbirds. Because they eat rodents and insects, they are a valuable asset to the garden.

Chimney Swift
(Swift Family)

Swifts are distinguishable from swallows in flight by their very slender, long, curved wings and stiff, short, stubby tails. Swallows are much more like other songbirds in form. Little can be done to attract chimney swifts, although they sometimes fly about the garden on their daily insect hunt. Some people consider their propensity to roost or nest in chimneys a nuisance, but most consider it fortunate if swifts choose their chimney for a home, for they consume enormous quantities of flying insects.

Habitat: The Chimney Swift can be found almost anywhere in its range because its chief habitat is the open sky. It is not a perching bird—it lives entirely on the wing except when roosting or on the nest. A strong flier, it ranges far and wide on its daily hunts. If the approach is open enough, a large pool or pond in the garden may be used for bathing and drinking on the wing.

Nesting: Formerly, Chimney Swifts nested in the hollow stumps of trees, but now they nest almost exclusively in manmade

structures. They grasp and break off twigs for their nests while on the wing. These twigs are cemented together and attached to the side of a vertical surface with a gluey saliva. Chimney Swifts frequently nest in large colonies in inactive industrial chimneys, farm silos and barns, and open wells, but they may also nest in single pairs in the smaller chimney of a home. At dusk, large migratory flocks enter their roost in a great spiraling funnel that is a dramatic sight.

Feeding: Swifts eat nothing but flying insects, which they catch on the wing. We can do little to provide food for them.

Ruby-throated Hummingbird
(Hummingbird Family)

For more information on attracting and feeding hummingbirds, see page 34.

This pugnacious bird has been known to attack and drive off other birds as large as hawks and crows. It is the only hummingbird that breeds in the eastern United States, and the only one we are likely to encounter in gardens there. Males have a brilliant, metallic-red throat that can appear black in the shade

or at certain angles; females have a white throat. Both have bright iridescent green backs and wings.

Habitat: The Ruby-throated Hummingbird is primarily a bird of woodland edges and openings, especially near brooks and streams where its favorite nectar plants grow. Many gardens are ideal habitats for this hummingbird, especially those with a margin of trees and shrubby borders surrounding a central lawn, with herbaceous borders and flower beds. Patios and decks are also excellent places to create this woodland opening effect. Running water, especially a gentle, trickling waterfall or a misty spray, is appreciated.

Nesting: The Ruby-throated Hummingbird constructs a tiny cup nest on the saddle of a horizontal twig or limb, made of plant down and spider webs, and camouflaged with bits of moss and lichen. It is usually located on the downsloping limb of a low tree, 5 to 25 feet above the ground, that overhangs a stream. It breeds from late March to

Anna's Hummingbird

Rufous Hummingbird

Red-headed Woodpecker

July, depending on how far north it resides.

Feeding: Flower nectar, lapped up by a brush-coated tongue extruded from its tubular bill, is the chief food of the Ruby-throated Hummingbird, but it also eats tiny insects and spiders. It has a strong preference for red, pink, or orange tubular flowers. Many garden plants are important sources of nectar, especially red columbine, scarlet sage, trumpet honeysuckle, petunia, phlox, bee balm, lilies, and trumpet creeper. It comes readily to hummingbird feeders stocked with sugar water.

Anna's Hummingbird
(Hummingbird Family)

This hummingbird is the only one that winters around its home range in the United States (mostly California). The male has bright red, metallic coloration on both the crown and the throat. Anna's Hummingbird is the most common garden hummingbird in California, and is readily attracted to hummingbird feeders.

Habitat: Chaparral and woodlands at the margins

of rivers and streams, especially where live oaks and scrub oaks predominate, are the favored habitat of this largely California hummingbird. Favorite garden habitats include shrubby borders and woodland edges heavy with suitable flowers.

Nesting: Anna's Hummingbird constructs a delicate little cup nest of plant down, spider webs, and bits of lichen and moss, placed on the saddle of a horizontal limb or twig in a shrub or low tree, in semi-shade. The nest is so small and so cleverly camouflaged that it is rarely noticed.

Feeding: Although it feeds largely on flower nectar, Anna's Hummingbird eats more tiny insects and spiders than do most other hummingbirds. It will also feed on sap from damaged trees and the holes left in trees by sapsuckers. Favorite nectar plants include eucalyptus, tree tobacco, century plant, and fuchsia. Anna's Hummingbird comes readily to hummingbird feeders.

Rufous Hummingbird
(Hummingbird Family)

This hummingbird can be observed in many gardens during its springtime flight northward from Mexico through the valleys of California, Oregon, and Wash-

ington, or on its July to September flight south through the western mountains. Males of this species are the only hummingbirds with reddish brown backs and tails. They have a scarlet-orange throat that, in the right light, may appear gold in color. Females have a green back and are virtually indistinguishable from the Allen's Hummingbird, whose range is a narrow strip along the California coast.

Habitat: This hummingbird breeds in mountain meadows and lowland forest edges and woodland openings, especially near running water. Garden habitats resembling woodland edges and openings, with a margin of trees and shrubby borders surrounding open lawn and flower beds, are most attractive, both during the breeding season and in migration. Rock gardens with alpine flowers make it feel quite at home.

Nesting: The Rufous Hummingbird builds a typical tiny hummingbird nest of plant down, spider webs, and lichen. Its preferred location is on the horizontal branch or twig of a conifer.

Feeding: This hummingbird is strongly attracted to

red flowers, and in fact will investigate nearly any bright red object. The Rufous Hummingbird loves crimson-flowered currant, red columbine, fuchsia, geranium, jasmine, trumpet vine, flowering citrus trees, penstemon, tiger lily, Indian paintbrush, and the white or pink flowers of the madrone tree or manzanita. It often comes to hummingbird feeders.

Red-headed Woodpecker
(Woodpecker Family)

Although it is still fairly common in parts of the Midwest and Southeast, the Red-headed Woodpecker has become a rare sight over much of its range in the last hundred years, partly because of intense nesting competition with starlings, and partly because it is more likely to be killed by automobiles

than most other birds. It can be distinguished by its entirely red head, neck, and upper breast. Large white patches set in black wings are a further aid to identification. Like the Red-bellied Woodpecker, it is fond of storing prodigious quantities of food that it may never use.

Habitat: This is a bird of open plains, fields, and pastures studded with scattered trees or shrubs. Open deciduous forest interrupted with burned or logged-over areas, and bottomland woods following rivers and streams, are favorite residences. It is frequently found in small towns and cities, along rural roads, and in open

Red-bellied Woodpecker

Yellow-bellied Sapsucker

country where there are many utility poles, upon which it often nests. Many gardens are attractive to the Red-headed Woodpecker, especially ones that have open areas of lawn and shrub beds with a few large trees, and that have an orchard, an open woodland grove, or some utility poles nearby. Dead or dying trees, or a few tall shrubs, are particularly attractive.

Nesting: Like most woodpeckers, this one excavates a cavity in which it lays eggs and raises its young, usually in the stump or large branch of a dead or dying deciduous tree. Where suitable nesting trees are not available, it may excavate a cavity in a utility pole or fencepost, or even under the roof of a house. Especially in areas with few dead trees, like many suburban and rural neighborhoods, nesting boxes are valuable to this bird. They are best mounted on tall posts or utility poles, out in the open, but near a grove or some large trees. Starlings compete aggressively with Red-headed Woodpeckers for nesting sites; in areas where starlings breed, it is advisable to set up an addi-

tional box for them.

Feeding: Unlike many other woodpeckers, the Red-headed Woodpecker seldom bores into trees for insects and larvae, although it may occasionally do so in dead stumps. Rather, it gleans insects off the bark while clinging to the trunk, and frequently forages for them on the ground or in shrubs. Its habit of catching flying insects on short loop flights from isolated trees frequently causes it to be struck by cars. Animal foods comprise about half of its diet overall, ranging from less than 10 percent in winter to over 65 percent in spring and summer. Acorns, corn, and beech nuts are important vegetable foods, along with wild berries (especially dogwood, serviceberry, tupelo, mountain ash, mulberry, brambles, and elderberries), and wild and cultivated fruits (strawberries, cherries, grapes, blueberries, and especially apples). This bird often comes to the feeder in winter, where it particularly enjoys suet, sunflower seeds, cracked corn, raisins, nutmeats, and baked goods.

Red-bellied Woodpecker
(Woodpecker Family)

This woodpecker is usually a nonmigratory permanent resident throughout its range. Although it used to be strictly a southeastern bird, it can now be found nesting as far north as southern Ontario. The Red-bellied Woodpecker is the most common woodpecker to visit feeding stations in the Southeast. Unlike the similar Golden-fronted Woodpecker of Texas, the Red-bellied Woodpecker's crown and nape are entirely scarlet. This bird stores huge quantities of food, to which it may not return.

Habitat: The Red-bellied Woodpecker prefers to live in deep to moderately open bottomland woods, especially swamp and flood plain woods along rivers and streams. It is also common in oak, pine, and mixed coniferous-deciduous woods. It is common in rural and suburban gardens, especially in the southeastern United States, wherever there are large old trees. Intensifying the "floodplain woods" habitats at the side of the street or along the drive may attract this bird.

Nesting: Favorite nesting

trees of this woodpecker include dead or dying maples, pines, willows, and elms. Rather than excavating its own cavity, the Red-bellied Woodpecker often uses manmade birdhouses.

Feeding: A large proportion of this woodpecker's diet is vegetable, but it can often be heard drilling into trees for beetles and insect larvae. It also forages for insects and vegetable food on the ground and in shrubs. Important wild vegetable foods include acorns, wild grapes, mulberries, wild cherries, pine seeds, hickory nuts; the fruits of Virginia creeper, poison ivy, bayberry, dogwood, elderberry, and palmetto; and the seeds and nuts of beech, hazelnut, and tupelo. It comes to the garden feeder in winter for suet, peanut butter mix, nutmeats, cracked corn, and sunflower seeds. Fruit is often taken in spring and summer.

Yellow-bellied Sapsucker
(Woodpecker Family)

The Yellow-bellied Sapsucker breeds from the Rocky Mountains and Great Basin ranges east to the Atlantic, and winters in the southern states and Mexico. It shows considerable variation in plumage. In general, it is a medium-sized woodpecker with a red crown and throat, a dull yellow underside, and

mottled black and white body. Two horizontal white stripes across the face and throat, and a white wing stripe, are distinguishing marks. The related Red-breasted Sapsucker breeds from the Sierras and Cascades to the coast in western North America; it resembles the eastern Red-headed Woodpecker in having an entirely red head, nape, and upper breast, but otherwise looks like the Yellow-bellied Sapsucker.

Habitat: These sapsuckers prefer mixed coniferous-deciduous forests, especially those near openings, logged-over groves of small deciduous trees, and wooded river bottoms and streamsides. All tend to breed in northern or mountainous areas where stands of aspen are common.

Nesting: Sapsuckers nest and raise their young in cavities they excavate in live aspen, birch, spruce, or cottonwood trees. They frequently start several nesting holes before completing one. They breed from April into June.

Feeding: Other woodpeckers are suspected of drilling holes for sap, but this is the only one that is known to use sap as a major food source. The

Downy Woodpecker

Northern Flicker

holes are drilled in a characteristic pattern of horizontal rows or a "checkerboard" network, just through the cambium layer of the bark of a wide variety of trees and shrubs. The cambium is eaten, as well as the energy-rich sap. Sapsuckers often return to the same sap wells many times, and they have been observed carrying sap in their beaks to their young. Many other species of birds and mammals eat the sap from the sapsucker holes, as well as the insects attracted to the sap, and for that reason alone they are an asset to the garden. Sapsuckers may damage trees by making them vulnerable to fungal organisms and insects, although this is controversial and little-documented. Although their holes are undeniably disfiguring to prized ornamentals, sapsuckers are seldom plentiful enough to do widespread damage. Besides sap, they eat many insects and larvae, and the fruits of holly, wild cherry, dogwood, Virginia creeper, red cedar, hackberry, elderberry, grape, sassafras, poison ivy, and poison oak. They are chiefly winter visitors to southern and lowland gardens, and are partial to suet, peanut butter mix, baked goods, and grape jelly, and will even take sugar water from hummingbird feeders.

Downy Woodpecker
(Woodpecker Family)

This is the smallest woodpecker in North America, about the size of a House Sparrow, and the only one (except for the similar but much larger Hairy Woodpecker) with a plain white back. Both sexes have white spots on black wings, but only males have the distinctive small bright red patch on the head. The Downy Woodpecker is the most common woodpecker to visit winter feeders throughout most of the United States.

Habitat: Woodlands broken up by logged patches, old fields and barns, waterside woods, and mixed coniferous-deciduous forests are favorite haunts of the Downy Woodpecker. It is a common resident almost anyplace that has a lot of trees, including suburban gardens, city parks, orchards, bottomland woods, and small woodlots. The most attractive gardens combine conifers and deciduous trees with open shrubby areas and groves of young deciduous trees. This bird is not found in coniferous forests or on western mountains.

Nesting: The Downy Woodpecker lays its eggs in a pear-shaped cavity that it excavates in a tree, usually a dead tree, stub, or stump, from 5 to 50 feet above the ground. Nests usually consist of a few chips of wood at the bottom of such holes. Suitable dead nesting trees, such as birches, poplars, aspens, and elms, are generally found in a stand of young deciduous trees, the offspring of the dead trees. The Downy Woodpecker will sometimes take up residence in a nesting box built to the appropriate dimensions.

Feeding: The Downy Woodpecker feeds chiefly on grubs, insects, and insect eggs that it chips out or pries loose while clinging to the bark of a tree trunk, limb, or twig. It also eats berries, especially those of poison ivy, dogwood, serviceberry, Virginia creeper, and tupelo; the seeds of apples, hornbeams, and sumac; and acorns, beechnuts, and walnuts. It is a common visitor to the garden feeder in winter, and is especially attracted by suet, peanut butter mix, and nutmeats. It also eats baked goods, especially corn bread, and cracked corn.

Northern Flicker
(Woodpecker Family)

Three forms of flickers, formerly thought to be separate species, are now known to be subspecies of the Northern Flicker. The Yellow-shafted subspecies is largely an eastern bird with yellow underneath the wings and tail. The Gilded subspecies is limited to the Southwest, largely southern Arizona and Mexico, and it too has yellow beneath the wings and tail. The Red-shafted subspecies is a western bird with scarlet or salmon wing and tail undersides. All Northern Flickers are woodpeckers, with brown backs that have black bars and spots, and dull whitish undersides with black spots. A crescent-shaped black spot on the breast is a distinguishing mark. The head is brown and gray, sometimes with red on the nape, and males have a black or red "whisker" mark.

Habitat: Flickers prefer open woods, old fields, and pastures with scattered shrubs, large trees, and open groves, as well as farmlands, logged-over woods, and woodland edges and openings. Woods following the course of rivers and streams in the plains states are also favorite habitats, as well as desert washes and deserts with giant saguaro cacti in the Southwest. In the garden, a mixture of large coniferous and deciduous trees with open areas of shrubby beds and groves of young deciduous trees is most appealing. Some open ground is a requirement.

Nesting: Flickers nest in cavities they excavate in the trunks or stubs of dead trees, almost always surrounded by shrubs or young saplings. They most often select old dead apple trees, sycamores, oaks, pines, and elms, but may also use many other trees. Where suitable dead or dying trees are scarce, they may nest in utility poles, fenceposts, the sides of barns, houses, and other buildings, and in saguaro cactus. Flickers readily use nesting boxes built to the appropriate dimensions, and mounted on a tall post over a dense planting of shrubs and small trees. Starlings compete aggressively with flickers for nest-

Black Phoebe

Eastern Phoebe

Purple Martin house

ing cavities; it is advisable to set out an additional box for starlings.

Feeding: Flickers eat an enormous amount of ants, which comprise almost half of their diet, as well as many other insects. They feed on the ground much of the time, but also on the trunks of trees. In spring and summer they eat animal food almost entirely; in fall and winter more than half of their food is vegetable, including wild fruits and berries (poison ivy, Virginia creeper, tupelo, hackberry, dogwood, wild cherry, brambles, grapes, blueberries, serviceberries, holly, red cedar, and bayberries) and the nuts and seeds of oak, sumac, grasses, clover, pigweed, ragweed, and mullein. Flickers often visit the winter feeder, where they eat suet, peanut butter mixture, and baked goods.

Black Phoebe
(Flycatcher Family)

Where this southwestern flycatcher inhabits valleys and coastal areas, it is generally a year-round resident. In harsher climates, especially at higher altitudes, it may migrate south for the winter. The Black Phoebe is sometimes confused with a junco, because of the clear, abrupt definition between its white underbelly and jet black body. A thin, flat bill

adapted to catching insects (compared to the cone-shaped, finchlike bill of juncos), upright posture while perching, and habitual tail-wagging distinguish it from juncos.

Habitat: The Black Phoebe is partial to waterside habitats, especially brooks, ponds, lakes, irrigation ditches, and canals under a canopy of trees. Garden pools, ponds, and streams, with their accompanying lush vegetation, are most attractive to this bird.

Nesting: The Black Phoebe attaches a mud nest mixed with twigs, grasses, and other fibrous plant materials to the rough wall of a cliff or bluff. Unlike that of the Eastern Phoebe, the nest is not supported on a ledge or shelf. Black Phoebes frequently nest on manmade structures, such as under eaves or bridges, or inside wells. They breed from March to August.

Feeding: These birds are insectivorous, darting down from a low perch in the branches of a tree, or a wall or fence, to snap up flying or crawling insects close to the ground, lawn, or surface of water.

Eastern Phoebe
(Flycatcher Family)

The Eastern Phoebe has adapted its breeding habitat to favor the structures of man that are near running water (especially bridges), over most of the eastern United States. It is an olive-gray bird with a white throat, dusty white underparts, and a thin, flattened black bill. Like the Black Phoebe, its tail-wagging while perched is a distinctive identifying trait. It is unlikely to visit the feeding station, but often nests in suitable gardens, especially near water.

Habitat: This bird distinctly prefers waterside habitats, and is most often found in wooded streamsides, including rocky ravines, and near bridges crossing streams. It is attracted by garden streams, pools with waterfalls, and other sources of running water.

Nesting: The Eastern Phoebe builds its nest on the ledges and in the crevices of the rocky walls of cliffs and ravines, or in caves. It often nests on manmade structures, under eaves, on the rafters of attics, sheds, and barns,

on windowsills, and most frequently on girders underneath bridges crossing streams. It often returns several years in a row to the same nesting spot. This bird will use a special nesting shelf built to the appropriate specifications and mounted under the eave of a house or porch near a suitable streamside habitat. It breeds from April to June.

Feeding: The Eastern Phoebe is almost entirely insectivorous in the spring, summer, and early fall. In winter, vegetable food may make up as much as 70 percent of its diet, including the fruits of sumac (a favorite), poison ivy, bayberries, holly, hackberries, blueberries, cherries, brambles, elderberries, and sassafras.

Purple Martin
(Swallow Family)

Best known for communal nesting in human-built "apartment houses," these musical aerial enthusiasts winter in South America, but frequently return to the same breeding spot year after year. The Purple Martin is the largest swallow in North America, and not purple as the name suggests, but blackish with metallic purple-blue highlights. Males are uniformly dark; females and young have gray or white underparts.

Habitat: The Purple Martin prefers grassy open

Tree Swallow

Cliff Swallow

Barn Swallow

streamsides, river bottom-lands and marshes, and meadows and large forest openings close to lakes and pools. The best garden habitats include open lawns and meadows near large bodies of water.

Nesting: Martins may nest in single pairs and small communities, but, especially in the eastern United States, prefer communities of eight or more pairs in close quarters. Originally, martins nested in holes and crevices in the sides of bluffs and cliffs, and in natural cavities and abandoned woodpecker holes in hollow stumps. On the West Coast, those are still their preferred nesting sites, as are abandoned woodpecker holes in the giant saguaro cacti of the Southwest. In the eastern United States, Purple Martins have learned to nest in gourds and special apartment houses set out by humans. Such birdhouses are the only means of attracting these birds, and must be placed in a suitable habitat.

Feeding: Martins consume vast quantities of insects on the wing, and are much sought after for controlling annoying insects. They have been reported to consume crumbled egg shells spread out on the ground for them during the nesting season.

Tree Swallow
(Swallow Family)

The clear, abrupt definition between its blackish, metallic blue, or blue-green upperparts and pure white underparts is a distinguishing feature of this bird. It readily nests in birdhouses, especially in gardens that are close to water.

Habitat: The Tree Swallow lives in a wide variety of waterside habitats, including wet meadows, marshes, swamps, and the shores of lakes, ponds, and streams.

Nesting: This bird prefers to nest in natural cavities and abandoned woodpecker holes in tree stumps. White chicken feathers are favorite nesting materials, along with grasses and straw. The nest is always located close to a body of water, preferably a stump jutting directly out of water, or overhanging it. Tree Swallows will also nest in boxes built to the appropriate dimensions. They are one of the few birds that will tolerate several close neighbors of their own species; nesting boxes can even be placed in the same tree. Tree Swallows breed from April to June, and are one of the

first birds to arrive North in their spring migration.

Feeding: Like other swallows, Tree Swallows feed largely on insects caught on the wing. Unlike their relatives, however, they often feed on fruits and berries, which can comprise as much as 30 percent of their diet in winter and early spring. Bayberries are especially favored, but they also eat the berries of red cedar, autumn olive, Virginia creeper, and dogwood, and the seeds of bullrushes, sedges, and smartweed.

Cliff Swallow
(Swallow Family)

Some people wish to discourage the Cliff Swallow's nests on their buildings; others try to attract them. But almost everyone admires the swift grace of a swallow in flight. The Cliff Swallow can be distinguished from the Barn Swallow in the air by its almost square tail. Up close, the crown, back, wings, and tail are glossy black, the throat and face brownish red, the rump pale or rusty buff, and the belly and forehead white.

Habitat: Like the Barn Swallow, the Cliff Swallow needs open country over

which to hunt on the wing, usually near bodies of water and the cliffs, dams, and large manmade structures upon which it nests. In the garden, they are attracted by open lawns near large bodies of water and agricultural land.

Nesting: The Cliff Swallow builds gourd-shaped nests of mud reinforced with grasses and other fibrous plant material, which it adheres to a vertical surface. Suitable nesting sites include the walls of cliffs and gorges, and of manmade structures, especially under the eaves of houses and barns. This is the swallow most often seen nesting under highway interchanges.

Feeding: The Cliff Swallow's diet consists almost entirely of insects caught on the wing.

Barn Swallow
(Swallow Family)

Some people consider swallows nesting on the walls of buildings a nuisance, but many more admire the spectacular grace of these birds in flight, and appreciate their consumption of enormous quantities of flying insects. This is the only North American swallow with a deeply forked tail. The topside of this bird is dark blue, and

the underparts are rufous to buff white, but coloration is seldom useful for identification, as Barn Swallows are generally seen in silhouette against the sky. They winter in South America, as far south as Argentina.

Habitat: Barn Swallows can be found in nearly any open country, often but not always close to water. Meadows, golf courses, parks, large lawns, pastures, and agricultural fields are favorite haunts. The best garden habitats include open lawns close to bodies of water.

Nesting: Originally the Barn Swallow adhered its nests to holes and crevices in the sides of caves, cliffs, and streambanks, but now they nest chiefly on the sides of manmade structures, under the eaves of barns, other farm outbuildings, and houses, and on the girders and rafters of bridges and buildings. Attaching a horizontal 2 x 4 with its narrow side facing up against a building will help encourage them to nest. To discourage them, knock down the nests as soon as the birds

Steller's Jay

Blue Jay

Scrub Jay

start to build them, throughout the breeding season, or place cloth or wire mesh over the eaves where they nest.

Feeding: Barn Swallows feed exclusively on insects they catch while flying. They are tireless fliers and may range far on their daily hunts, which usually perform socially. They drink and bathe on the wing, dipping into large pools, rivers, and other bodies of water.

Steller's Jay
(Crow Family)

This jay is less likely to visit gardens in the West than is the Scrub Jay, as it prefers deep forests. Its sooty black crest and head, and cobalt-blue body, wings, and tail are a familiar sight around campgrounds and parks. The Steller's Jay is the western counterpart of the eastern Blue Jay in temperament and behavior.

Habitat: This is mostly a bird of deep coniferous forests, including higher elevations, but it also inhabits mixed coniferous-deciduous forests. In fall and winter it frequently moves into the more open oak woods of lowlands, and even into the open woodlands of the western prairie states. Western gardens with many large conifers and oaks, particularly those near forests, are attractive to this jay.

Nesting: The Steller's Jay builds a neat but bulky nest of sticks and twigs cemented together with mud and lined with grasses and fine plant rootlets. The nest is usually placed on the forked branch of a dense, shady conifer. The breeding season is from April to July.

Feeding: These birds feed from the high treetops to the ground. Most of their diet is vegetable, but they also eat insects (mostly bees and wasps), and sometimes plunder the nests of songbirds for eggs and young. Their most important food is acorns, but pine seeds, grains, (oats, wheat, barley, and corn), and fruits and berries (elderberries, cherries, brambles, dogwood, and many others), are major foods too. Bird feeders

well stocked with sunflower seeds, nutmeats, and finely cracked corn are frequently visited by Steller's Jays.

Blue Jay
(Crow Family)

Like crows, Blue Jays sound the alarm against predators for the whole bird community. They may monopolize feeders and drive off other birds. Blue Jays have the habit of carrying off seeds and acorns and "planting" them in storage caches in the ground. At feeders they prefer eating from the ground, although in the East they also come to platform feeders.

Habitat: Surprisingly, the Blue Jay was originally a cautious bird of deep forests, especially those dominated by oaks. Only since the first part of this century have they become common in rural and suburban gardens and city parks. They prefer gardens with a large number of older trees, especially oaks, beeches, and pines. They love to bathe, and a source of water is a major attraction.

Nesting: The Blue Jay's nest is a bulky cup of twigs and other plant materials, lined with grass and fine rootlets. It can be placed in the crotch of any of a variety of trees and shrubs, usually in a woodland of oaks and beeches, but sometimes in a conifer. The parents aggressively defend the nest against intruders, including humans. Blue Jays breed from March into July, and sometimes later in the southern states. During breeding, the Blue Jay's quiet, skulking behavior differs radically from its usual raucous, mischievous antics.

Feeding: During winter and fall, Blue Jays eat an almost entirely vegetable diet. Acorns are their most important food, followed by beech nuts and waste corn. Other nuts, such as hickory, walnuts, and filberts; many seeds and fruits; and most berries are also attractive. In the spring and summer they eat many insects, and sometimes small reptiles, rodents, songbirds, and the eggs and young of birds. Animal foods at that time make up about 40 percent of the Blue Jay's diet. A familiar guest at winter feeders, these birds are especially fond of whole peanuts and sunflower seeds. Black and gray striped sunflower seeds are much preferred over the oil-type. Suet is also a favorite. Corn is only moderately attractive.

Scrub Jay
(Crow Family)

This large, blue and white, crestless bird has much the same disposition as the eastern Blue Jay. It is perhaps a little more shy, but quickly gets used to humans nearby and reveals its characteristic raucous behavior. It is commonly found around gardens and bird feeders in the West, and in scattered locations in Florida.

Habitat: Oak woodlands and chaparral are the haunts of the Scrub Jay. It avoids low chaparral and scrub, where surveillance perches are uncommon. It is a frequent visitor and breeding resident of western gardens, particularly where dense shrubs and oaks predominate.

Nesting: Scrub Jays build bulky nests of sticks and twigs lined with grasses and fine plant rootlets, in shrubs or low trees. They breed from March into July and earlier in their small range in Florida.

American Crow

Black-capped Chickadee

Feeding: These birds feed almost entirely on the ground, and occasionally in the low branches of a shrub. About 60 percent of their diet in spring and summer, and 80 percent in fall and winter, is vegetable, consisting largely of nuts (especially acorns and pinyon pine seeds) and many fruits and berries (brambles, currants, elderberries, manzanita berries, blueberries, cherries, and plums). Waste corn and wheat are also important foods. In spring and summer they eat a wide variety of insects, small reptiles, small rodents, and sometimes the eggs and young of songbirds. Scrub Jays are frequent but cautious visitors to feeding stations, especially for nutmeats, sunflower seeds, finely cracked corn, and bakery crumbs.

American Crow
(Crow Family)

These familiar shiny black birds are extremely adaptable and intelligent. They perform many valuable services and do not really deserve the "bad press" they frequently receive. They are very social, nesting relatively close together and traveling in winter flocks that can number in the hundreds or even thousands. They often collect and hoard bright objects, and have a complex communication system, including expert mimicry. Crows provide a service to the whole animal community by acting as wary sentries, alerting the world to possible danger with their raucous calls, and often mob and drive away predators, especially hawks and owls.

Habitat: Human alteration of the landscape has encouraged the proliferation of crows, as some of their favorite habitats include farmlands, roadsides, highways, suburban areas, thinned or logged-over forests, and orchards. Open forests, and woodlands along the margins of rivers and streams, are favorite natural habitats. Open, treeless plains and deserts are usually avoided by crows, but the planting of windbreaks and gardens in such country has expanded their range. Crows are very adaptable, and live essentially wherever there are trees.
Nesting: Crows build sturdy nests of sticks and twigs, lined with a variety of plant materials, and placed in the tops of trees. Open woods are favorite

nesting spots, but sometimes a lone tree or even the crossarms of a utility pole are used. Rarely, when trees are not available, they will nest in shrubs or even on the ground. They often nest in loose colonies. The breeding season is from February through June.
Feeding: Crows are much maligned for the damage they supposedly cause to grain crops. Actually, while grain is an important food to these birds, most of what they eat is waste grain picked up from the ground after the harvest. They also eat an immense number of damaging insects in fields, orchards, and gardens. Plant foods, including grains (especially corn, wheat, buckwheat, and oats) and many berries, nuts, and fruits (mulberries, cherries, sumac, brambles, poison ivy, bayberries, dogwood, serviceberries, acorns, and pecans) comprise about half their diet in spring and summer, and about 80 percent in fall and winter. Animal foods include a huge variety of insects, small reptiles, and crustaceans. Crows also scavenge gar-

bage, dead fish along rivers and streams, and other dead animals along highways. As scavengers they play an important clean-up role for man and natural communities alike. They plunder the nests of many songbirds, eating both eggs and nestlings, and thus are often despised by bird lovers. Crows are very cautious around bird feeders, rarely bold enough to eat anywhere but on the ground away from the house. They love grain (especially corn), bread crumbs and other bakery products, and suet. If crows come to your feeders in winter, be sure that the suet is well-attached or they will fly off with quite large pieces.

Black-capped Chickadee
(Titmouse Family)

Although the Black-capped Chickadee is mostly a permanent resident in its range, some individuals fly a little south of the breeding range (the north-central states) for the winter. The black crown and bib and white cheeks of this small gray and white

bird are familiar in many gardens in the winter.

Habitat: The Black-capped Chickadee prefers mixed coniferous-deciduous forests typical of the northern United States and southern Canada. Isolated woodland groves and thickets of deciduous shrubs at the edges and openings of coniferous forests are also favorite spots. They often take up residence in suburban gardens, especially when dense plantings of shrubs and young sapling thickets are backed by mature deciduous and coniferous trees.
Nesting: Chickadees are cavity-nesting birds, sometimes nesting in abandoned woodpecker holes and the natural cavities of trees. Most often they dig their own nesting holes out of partially rotted tree trunks or stumps, usually birch or pine. They will occasionally use bird boxes built to the appropriate specifications. Lining the nesting box with

Chestnut-backed Chickadee

Tufted Titmouse

Plain Titmouse

small wood chips may persuade them to use it. They won't use the chips for nesting, carrying them away instead, but such a lining seems to convince them that the nesting box is fresh and acceptable. Chickadees move from forest edges and openings to dense woods for nesting, and birdhouses should be placed in a similar habitat. Mount the box on the trunk of a pine, birch, aspen, or elm tree, or preferably on a rotting snag.

Feeding: The Black-capped Chickadee is largely an insect-eater. In spring and summer its diet includes only about 10 percent plant foods, but this can rise to over 50 percent in winter. Constantly active, it characteristically hops around and clings to twigs, branches, and foliage, gleaning huge quantities of insect eggs and larvae from twigs and bark, and snapping up a wide variety of insects from foliage and sometimes from the air. Pine seeds are an important natural vegetable food, along with the seeds and nuts of hemlock, birch, pine, walnut, ragweed, and sunflower, and the berries of poison ivy, blueberry, bayberry, and serviceberry. During the nonbreeding season chickadees travel in well-organized flocks, often joined by Downy Woodpeckers, Tufted Titmice, kinglets, Brown Creepers, and nuthatches.

These other birds may take advantage of the chickadees' keen ability to spot food and predators. Chickadees come regularly to feeding stations, where oil-type sunflower seeds are their preferred food, followed by black-striped, then gray-striped sunflower seeds. They will also eat peanut kernels and other nutmeats, hulled sunflower seeds, peanut butter mix, and suet. Chickadees seem to prefer wobbly, hanging feeders that few other birds will use. They also come to platform and window feeders, suet feeders, and sometimes even hummingbird feeders.

Related Species: The Carolina Chickadee is the southeastern counterpart of the Black-capped Chickadee, to which it is very similar in appearance. When its wings are folded, the feathers of the Carolina Chickadee show less white on the edges. The two species occupy almost identical niches and seldom overlap ranges, especially during the breeding season. The range of the Carolina Chickadee extends from southwestern Kansas through central Missouri, Illinois, Indiana, and Ohio, to parts of southwestern and southeastern Pennsylvania, central New Jersey, and south to the Gulf Coast from eastern Texas to central Florida.

Chestnut-backed Chickadee
(Titmouse Family)

Similar to the Black-capped Chickadee, except that it has a bright, reddish brown back and sides, and a blackish brown cap, this chickadee is common throughout the forested Northwest. It is as inquisitive and sharp at spotting food as are its eastern relatives.

Habitat: The Chestnut-backed Chickadee prefers moist, coniferous forests, especially the rain forests of the Pacific coast. It also inhabits woods at the margins of streams, and similar habitats in gardens. Tall, mature trees and dark woodlands, from dense stands of conifers to eucalyptus, are the key to attracting this bird.

Nesting: Chestnut-backed Chickadees nest in natural cavities, in abandoned woodpecker holes, or in holes they dig out in rotting trees, usually firs. They often use nesting boxes. They breed from March to June.

Feeding: Like other chickadees, these birds are mostly insectivorous, but up to 40 percent of their diet in winter is vegetable.

Pine seeds are their most important natural plant food, followed by poison oak berries. They also eat thimbleberries and Pacific wax myrtle. At the feeding station, sunflower seeds and suet are their favorite foods; they will sometimes eat finely cracked corn and apples. Where the range of this bird overlaps with that of the Black-capped Chickadee, it confines itself to foraging in tall trees, usually conifers, while the Black-capped Chickadee generally feeds lower, in streamside thickets or oaks. Like all chickadees, winter flocks of this species are usually accompanied by a variety of other small birds.

Tufted Titmouse
(Titmouse Family)

This small, gray, crested bird is a frequent visitor to the winter feeder, and is

especially welcome for its jaunty, active disposition. It is a permanent resident throughout its range, expanding its home range in winter.

Habitat: The Tufted Titmouse breeds and lives most of its life in deciduous woods, preferring those in bottomlands, swamps, and riversides. It is most common in gardens in winter (perhaps because it is more conspicuous in leafless trees), but may reside there the year round if a dense cover of deciduous trees is available.

Nesting: The Tufted Titmouse nests in the natural cavities of trees and abandoned woodpecker holes,

Bushtit

Red-breasted Nuthatch

and will often use a nesting box built to the proper dimensions. Place the nesting box on a tree trunk, or on a fence post in semishade. The nest is constructed of moss, leaves, plant fibers, and animal hair of many kinds. Placing hair (horse hair, combings from pets, or human hair) in suet feeders may entice titmice to nest nearby.

Feeding: Like their relatives the chickadees, titmice are largely insectivorous, especially in spring, summer, and fall. In winter over 70 percent of their diet may be plant foods, especially acorns, beechnuts, hickory nuts, walnuts, and pine seeds, but also including many other berries and seeds. Brambles are among their favorite fruits, as are mulberries, elderberries, serviceberries, bayberries, and grapes. At the bird feeder, peanut kernels are their favorite food, with black-striped and gray-striped sunflower seeds in second place. They will also eat oil-type sunflower seeds, and are attracted to suet and peanut butter mix. Titmice hunt for insects by clinging to twigs and branch tips, and sometimes they cling to trunks and peer into bark crevices. Hanging feeders, suet feeders mounted on tree trunks, and suet or peanut butter mix smeared directly onto trunks and branches are excellent methods of feeding them.

Plain Titmouse
(Titmouse Family)

The western counterpart to the Tufted Titmouse, the Plain Titmouse is also small, gray, and crested, and shares the same inquisitive, vivacious disposition. It is a permanent resident through its range.

Habitat: This bird prefers oak woodlands, but also inhabits pinyon and juniper woodlands and a variety of deciduous woods, thickets, and shrublands with scattered trees. Streamsides and forest edges are especially attractive, but the Plain Titmouse is a very adaptable bird, and is a frequent garden resident.

Nesting: Like the Tufted Titmouse, the Plain Titmouse nests in the cavities of trees, sometimes in natural holes and those abandoned by woodpeckers, and sometimes in holes it excavates itself in a rotting trunk or stump. Fencepost holes, cavities in old buildings, and nesting boxes built to the proper specifications are sometimes chosen. Attract breeding birds by setting out hair, bits of fur, feathers, and thread for nest building. The breeding season is from March to July.

Feeding: The Plain Titmouse feeds mostly by clinging to twigs and limbs of trees and shrubs, but also forages on the ground. It is mostly insectivorous in spring and summer, and mostly vegetarian in winter. Important plant foods include acorns, cherries, pine seeds, walnuts, apples, thistle, and oats. At the feeder its tastes are similar to those of the Tufted Titmouse: peanut kernels, sunflower seeds, suet, and peanut butter.

Bushtit
(Bushtit Family)

These western birds, which often nest and feed around gardens, are permanent residents throughout their range. Abundant water is the best way to attract them. Among the smallest birds in North America, bushtits are dark gray with a lighter gray underside, and have a long gray tail and a very short bill. During most of the year they travel about in noisy, cheerful flocks.

Habitat: Bushtits prefer bushy, deciduous streamside vegetation, like alder and willow thickets; woodland edges of maples and dogwoods; and chaparral, pinyon, juniper, and scrub oak woodlands. They often inhabit western gardens, especially where shrubs and groves of young deciduous trees are dominant. Thick vegetation with water for bathing and drinking is the best way to persuade Bushtits to live in your garden.

Nesting: This bird constructs an interesting, sacklike, gourd-shaped nest with an entrance hole near the top. The nest is often hung in plain sight in small trees or shrubs. Bushtits breed from April to July. Normally gregarious and traveling in flocks, they are paired and shy during the breeding season.

Feeding: Although they are mostly insectivorous, Bushtits do occasionally eat berries and fruits, mostly of poison oak. There is some evidence that leaf galls are their chief vegetable food. Hopping and flitting about on leaves and twigs of shrubs and low trees, frequently in flocks of up to 50 individuals, they glean enormous quantities of aphids, beetles, scale nits, leafhoppers, and many other insects. They are not known to take food from feeding stations, but frequently come to garden water sources to bathe.

Red-breasted Nuthatch
(Nuthatch Family)

This constantly active bird can often be seen creeping downward on tree trunks, clinging with its stiff tail and sharp claws, which are especially adapted to trunk climbing. A distinctive black stripe across the eye and a rust-colored breast distinguish this bird, along with its habit of clinging to the cones of conifers and deftly extracting the seeds.

Habitat: The Red-breasted Nuthatch is a bird of forests that have plenty of conifers, including strictly coniferous forests, and mixed coniferous-deciduous forests. Its generally northern range has been gradually extended southward by the increasing use of ornamental conifers in gardens. Relatively mature stands of conifers attract this bird to the garden year-round.

Nesting: This cavity-nesting bird generally digs

White-breasted Nuthatch

Brown Creeper

Cactus Wren

its own nesting hole out of the soft, decaying wood of a dead tree, especially pine, aspen, birch, or fir. It characteristically smears the entrance hole with pitch (the sticky sap exuded from the damaged bark of a conifer), which often gives its feathers a messy look. Red-breasted Nuthatches also nest in woodpecker holes and in nesting boxes built to the correct specifications and hung on the trunk of a tree (preferably a dead one) about 15 feet above the ground. Nuthatch nests are loosely constructed; never open the bird box while it is occupied, or everything may fall out. They breed from April to June.
Feeding: Red-breasted Nuthatches feed primarily on the seeds of conifers and on insects gleaned from the bark of tree trunks. They also sometimes feed on the ground, or while clinging to the seedheads of herbaceous plants like ragweed or sunflowers. In the garden, they are attracted to beech, elder, and Virginia creeper. They often store food for hard times. Attract them to the winter feeder with suet, peanut butter mix, peanut kernels, nutmeats, and sunflower seeds.

White-breasted Nuthatch
(Nuthatch Family)

More common at feeders and more widespread than its smaller, red-breasted relative, this inquisitive nuthatch is most readily identified by its habit of creeping down tree trunks and stopping occasionally with its head held at a 90 degree angle, and by its plain white underparts, black crown and nape, and white face without a stripe across the eye. It is quite tame around feeders, and can even be taught to accept food from human hands.

Habitat: White-breasted Nuthatches can be found virtually anywhere there are forests. In the West they inhabit pine forests as readily as oak or juniper woodlands. In the East they prefer primarily deciduous woods, especially those with beeches or oaks.
Nesting: White-breasted Nuthatches nest in the natural cavities and knotholes of dead trees, or in abandoned woodpecker holes.

Occasionally they excavate a nesting hole themselves in the soft wood of dead or decaying trees. Oaks, elms, maples, apple, and other deciduous trees are prime candidates; pine trees are also used. White-breasted Nuthatches often use nesting boxes built to the correct dimensions and mounted at least 15 feet up in a tree in a woodland setting. They breed from March to June.
Feeding: Insects gleaned from the bark of tree trunks, and the nuts of deciduous trees (especially acorns and beechnuts), are the principle natural foods of the White-breasted Nuthatch. It clings in any position and moves up or down freely, occasionally descending to the ground. Especially in the West, but also in its eastern range, pine seeds, waste grains (corn, wheat, oats), and the seeds and berries of other plants are important supplements. The White-breasted Nuthatch stores food in the fall under the loose bark of trees. It is a frequent visitor to winter feeding stations for suet and sunflower seeds, and also for peanut butter mix, nutmeats, and sometimes finely cracked corn and millet.

Brown Creeper
(Creeper Family)

The feeding behavior of this active, amusing bird is its hallmark; clinging to

the trunks of trees and large limbs with its long, sharp claws, it spirals upward around the trunk (never facing downward or sideways), probing the bark for insects, until it nears the top of the tree, then flies down to the base of another tree to repeat the performance. A small bird with a mottled brown back and long, down-curved bill, it has a stiff tail with which it braces itself while clinging to a vertical support. It is the only creeper in North America.

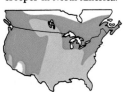

Habitat: Any type of forest is a suitable habitat for this bird, which is populous in the northern parts of its range. It is attracted to densely wooded gardens with large, mature trees. The shagbark hickory is an excellent tree to attract them.
Nesting: Sometimes creepers nest in natural cavities or abandoned woodpecker holes in dead trees, but more often they build their nests under loose, shaggy bark like that found on dead trees and the live shagbark hickory. Creepers are difficult to entice into a nesting box.
Feeding: Most of the Brown Creeper's diet consists of insects gleaned from the bark of trees, al-

though it does consume some nuts and seeds. In winter it enjoys peanut butter mix spread on the bark of trees, as well as chopped peanut kernels.

Cactus Wren
(Wren Family)

The Cactus Wren is easily distinguished from other wrens by its large size (the largest of all wrens, it is as big as a Starling), its speckled breast (the dark spots concentrate on the upper breast), and a long tail that is never cocked at right angles. It often takes up residence in gardens and around human habitations in the arid Southwest.

Habitat: A chief requirement for Cactus Wrens is plenty of prickly, thorny shrubs and cacti in which to nest. Dense scrub along watercourses is a favorite home, along with sunny hillsides adjoining mesas and foothills. These birds are permanent residents throughout their range, and seldom wander from their established home territory.
Nesting: Cactus Wren nests are shaped like a bottle with a crooked neck, with the narrow entrance hole and tunnel off to one

House Wren

Carolina Wren

Winter Wren

side. They are often so embedded in and surrounded with prickles and thorns that one wonders how the bird uses them without injury. Cholla cactus, prickly pear, and catclaw bushes are favorites, but many other thorny plants are used as well. Occasionally these wrens nest in abandoned woodpecker holes in trees, or in cavities in old buildings. A Cactus Wren's home territory often includes dozens of nests; each spring and summer new nests are built, usually one for each of two or three broods, but old ones are kept in repair for roosting. They seldom use nest boxes.

Feeding: Only about 10 percent of the Cactus Wren's diet is vegetable food, especially the fruits of prickly pear and elderberry. Most of its food consists of insects it forages on the ground, picking up leaves, sticks, and other objects and searching underneath. Cactus Wrens occasionally visit feeding stations for bread crumbs.

Carolina Wren
(Wren Family)

The rich reddish brown of its upperparts and conspicuous white stripe across the eye characterize this bird, the largest wren in its eastern range. Carolina Wrens will nest in practically any cavity avail-

able, from the pocket of an old discarded coat to a lidless tin can.

Habitat: Brushy undergrowth is the favorite habitat of Carolina Wrens. They also inhabit rocky slopes thick with brush and thickets, shrubby forest edges and deeper undergrowth, and isolated groups of shrubs and trees in midwestern plains and moist lowlands. Woody gardens with a dense understory of shrubs are most attractive. These birds are permanent residents throughout their range, and are sometimes killed by cold weather at the northernmost fringes.
Nesting: Carolina Wrens prefer cavities for nesting, although they sometimes nest in the crotches of trees. They are quite inventive about finding suitable cavities but will often nest in boxes built especially for them. They breed from April to July, and often raise two broods.
Feeding: Insects are the chief fare of the Carolina Wren. Only about 10 percent of its diet is plant food, and that is mostly in winter. Suet, peanut butter mix, sunflower seeds, nutmeats, and corn bread will occasionally attract them to the feeder in winter.

House Wren
(Wren Family)

Sometimes confused with the slightly smaller Winter Wren, the House Wren is much more common around human dwellings. A plain gray brown, this bird is distinguished by its small size, jaunty wagging tail that is frequently held at a right angle to its body, and a cocky, vivacious personality during the breeding season.

Habitat: Lowland deciduous woods, and shrubby woodland edges and openings are the best places to find this bird. It often takes up residence in gardens, particularly those with a backdrop of trees and shrubs surrounding a lawn or patio. House Wrens are migratory.
Nesting: The early-arriving male constructs many trial nests in anticipation of attracting a mate. Usually the nest she selects will be completely torn apart and reconstructed from scratch, often with the same materials. House Wrens build their nests in cavities of an astounding variety, from old shoes or the interior of a discarded living room sofa to the more prosaic sites of natu-

ral tree cavities and abandoned woodpecker holes. They readily nest in boxes built to the correct dimensions, and are among the few birds that will nest in a birdhouse or hollow gourd dangling from a tree limb or a wire. Because of the male's nest-building ambitions, a number of wren boxes in the garden are appreciated, although only one is eventually used to raise each brood; the nesting territory is usually about 1/2 to 3/4 of an acre. House Wrens have been known to visit the nests of neighboring wrens and songbirds and pierce the eggs.
Feeding: House Wrens feed almost entirely on insects. Suet, corn bread, and white bread crumbs may attract them to the feeder in spring and summer, although only rarely.

Winter Wren
(Wren Family)

Quite similar to the House Wren in appearance, the Winter Wren is smaller, darker, and usually has a shorter tail. It is also shier and less likely to frequent gardens.

Habitat: The Winter Wren's chief habitat is the dark, shady undergrowth of coniferous forests, especially along steep lush stream banks. Gardens most likely to attract this shy bird are those near large, mature coniferous forests, and that are themselves dense woodlands.
Nesting: The Winter Wren's nest is cunningly

Ruby-crowned Kinglet

Eastern Bluebird

Hermit Thrush

concealed on or near the ground, usually among the roots of a fallen tree, or under the roots of stumps, on streambanks or roadcuts, and occasionally in abandoned buildings. Although most are migratory, some individuals remain in their harsh northern breeding range the year round, so roosting boxes in winter are especially attractive. Winter Wrens have been known to use nesting boxes placed low against the side of a shed or stump, but this is not common. Males commonly build one or more "decoy" nests out in the open.

Feeding: These birds feed almost exclusively on insects, but may come to winter feeders for bread crumbs.

Ruby-crowned Kinglet
(Old World Warbler/ Thrush Family)

The two kinglets are among the smallest birds in North America, along with hummingbirds and bushtits. The Ruby-crowned Kinglet is the more likely to visit feeders in its southern

winter range, and is distinguished from the Golden-crowned Kinglet, vireos, and wood warblers by its red crown patch (males only, and usually concealed unless the bird is excited), its nervous flickering of wings while it moves from twig to twig, and its habit of hovering in front of twigs and leaves as it inspects them for food.

Habitat: This bird seldom visits gardens in spring and summer, choosing dense coniferous forests instead. In winter it migrates to coastal and southern states, where deciduous and coniferous thickets and forest edges are its domain.

Nesting: The Ruby-crowned Kinglet nests in northern and high-altitude coniferous forests. It builds a hanging, globular nest, suspended from the tip of a branch high up in a spruce, fir, or other conifer. It breeds from May to July.

Feeding: Flitting from spot to spot, this tiny bird is well adapted to foraging on the delicate tips of branches for aphids, scales, and other tiny insects and their eggs. It is almost entirely insectivorous, although it occasionally eats a few nuts, seeds, or small fruits. It may visit small hanging feeders stocked with suet, peanut butter mix, and finely chopped nutmeats.

Related Species: The Golden-crowned Kinglet, which is even tinier than the similar Ruby-crowned Kinglet, is distinguished by its orange-yellow crown. While it has a broader winter range than the Ruby-crowned Kinglet, it is less likely to visit winter feeders. When it does, it is frequently found in mixed flocks which include chickadees. Like the Ruby-crowned Kinglet, it seldom nests near human habitations.

Eastern Bluebird
(Old World Warbler/ Thrush Family)

This popular harbinger of spring is difficult to mistake, with its bright blue upperparts, reddish breast, and white belly. Competition for nesting sites with European Starlings and House Sparrows has been

an important factor in greatly reducing its population.

Habitat: Bluebirds are commonly found in old fields with scattered trees and open, second-growth woodlands. Other favorite spots are orchards, especially apple orchards, open farmlands with a few trees, and fencerows. The logging of the eastern American forests has done much to expand the range of this bird, although it has recently experienced a population downturn. Rural gardens and orchards, and suburban gardens near open farmlands, are ideal places to attract bluebirds. Scattered trees, especially fruit trees, mixed with open lawn and herbaceous flower beds, make an excellent garden habitat.

Nesting: Bluebirds nest in natural cavities in trees, and in old woodpecker holes in trees and fenceposts. They readily use nesting boxes built to the correct dimensions. Providing birdhouses to supplement these scarce natural sites is an important way we can help to

halt the decline of this beautiful bird. A 1½-inch entrance hole will exclude starlings but not House Sparrows. Place the nesting box low to the ground (4 to 5 feet) to discourage the more wary House Sparrow. Keep the bluebird nesting box as far from human habitations and activities as possible. Mounting it on a fence post or utility pole (with proper permission) is best; small trees in full sun are next best. Don't mount the boxes on the trunks of large trees. Roadsides, pastures, and woodland edges facing open land are the best locations. Bluebirds are strongly territorial, and will constantly fight with each other if their nests are too close together. Three nesting boxes may be squeezed into a 1-acre garden, however, if they are placed at least 400 feet apart, and preferably away from and on opposite sides of the house, garage, or other large obstruction.

Feeding: Bluebirds eat large quantities of insects, which make up over 80 percent of their diet in spring and summer, and about 60 percent in their southerly winter range. They perch on fence posts or small trees and fly down to eat on the grassy ground. They eat the berries and fruits of dogwood, red cedar, sumac, bayberry, Virginia creeper, holly, blueberry, hackberry, and elderberry. Peanut butter mix, chopped

Wood Thrush

American Robin

dried fruit, and chopped peanut kernels attract them to southern hanging feeders in winter.

Related Species: The Western Bluebird is the counterpart of the Eastern Bluebird, from southern British Columbia and central Montana south to Mexico. Like the Eastern Bluebird, it lives in open parklands, pastures and fields with scattered trees, forest edges and clearings, and gardens, and often uses nesting boxes. Competition for nesting sites with European Starlings, Violet-green Swallows, and House Wrens, plus an increasing scarcity of suitable nesting cavities, has resulted in population decline.

Hermit Thrush
(Old World Warbler/ Thrush Family)

This is the only spotted thrush that winters in the United States, so it is the only one likely to visit winter feeding stations. Dull brown upperparts and a usually rufous rump and tail distinguish this bird from other thrushes with spotted breasts. During spring and summer it is a shy, secretive bird of wilder forests.

Habitat: Deciduous woodlands and thickets, especially with berry bushes, are the winter habitats of this bird, and a dense cover of shrubs and trees is necessary to make it comfortable in the garden. In spring and summer it moves to the more remote habitats of mixed deciduous-coniferous woods and purely coniferous forests. Especially in the Northwest it nests at higher altitudes, frequently near the timberline.

Nesting: The cup nest of the Hermit Thrush is usually built directly on the ground, under a small conifer or shrub, at the edge of woods. The breeding season is from May to August.

Feeding: In spring and summer the Hermit Thrush feeds mostly on insects foraged on the ground, but in winter plant foods constitute about 60 percent of its diet. Fleshy fruits and berries are the major vegetable sources, especially the fruits of holly, cotoneaster, pyracantha, dogwood, serviceberry, sumac, and grape, and toyon, madrone, peppertree, and poison oak in the West. At the feeder, Hermit Thrushes divide their time about equally between ground feeders and low platform feeders. They enjoy suet, peanut butter mix, nutmeats, raisins, sliced apples, and bakery crumbs.

Wood Thrush
(Old World Warbler/ Thrush Family)

Distinguished by bold black spots on its breast and a bright rusty head, this thrush is the one most likely to nest in the garden. It migrates to southern Mexico and Central America for the winter. Some consider its song the most beautiful of all birds'.

Habitat: Moist deciduous woods with a thick understory of small trees and shrubs, especially near streams and pools, are the favorite dwelling places of the Wood Thrush. A shy, secretive bird, it has recently adapted to nesting in gardens, where it remains more often heard than seen. Woodland gardens with a densely planted understory are prime locations for nesting. A shady ground-level bird bath with a close cover of shrubs is a distinct plus, as these birds love to bathe in seclusion.

Nesting: The nest of the Wood Thrush is quite similar to that of the American Robin, and is usually placed on the crotch or branch of a shrub or small tree 6 to 12 feet off the ground. The breeding season is from April to July.

Feeding: In spring the Wood Thrush feeds almost entirely on insects caught on the ground or picked off the foliage of trees or shrubs. As summer and fall approach, its diet gradually includes more and more plant food, up to about 75 percent at the time of migration. Fleshy fruits and berries are its favorites, topped by the fruits of spicebush, dogwood, cherry, grape, blackberry, tupelo, mulberry, Virginia creeper, and elderberry. Although it seldom visits the summer bird feeder, this thrush occasionally eats raisins and chopped dried prunes scattered on the ground, and suet placed in a sheltered, shady location.

American Robin
(Old World Warbler/ Thrush Family)

The familiar American Robin, with its gray upperparts and reddish breast, varying from pale rust to a dark brick red, is another popular songbird that has benefited from human alteration of the landscape. There is scarcely a garden in this country that has not been visited at least a few times by this successful bird.

Habitat: A bird of woodland edges and openings, the American Robin needs open ground on which it can forage for food, and some woods or at least a few scattered trees and shrubs for nesting and roosting. Gardens, particularly those with open lawns adjacent to woodlands, groves, and small trees and shrubs, are ideal. In winter, berry bushes are particularly attractive.

Nesting: Robins construct a cup nest, which the female lines with mud by smearing it on the inner bowl with her breast. The nest is usually placed in the crotch of a tree or shrub, from near the ground to as high as 50 feet. Windowsills and other

Wrentit

Gray Catbird

Northern Mockingbird

ledges on human structures, as well as special nesting shelves, are also used, as long as the site has a firm support and overhead protection from rain. The availability of mud at nesting time may entice these birds to nest nearby. They breed from April to July. In northern areas their first brood is usually raised in an evergreen tree or shrub, and later one or two broods in deciduous trees.

Feeding: Robins are most often observed foraging in lawns for earthworms. They also eat many insects, including caterpillars and beetle grubs. More than 60 percent of the robin's diet in summer, fall, and winter is composed of fleshy fruits and berries of both wild and cultivated plants. Berry bushes like pyracantha, which retain their fruits through the colder months, will attract robins in the nonbreeding seasons. They will sometimes come to feeding stations for bread crumbs.

Related Species: The Varied Thrush of the Pacific Northwest, a shy woodland bird sometimes mistaken for a robin, prefers the shady floor of a wet, coniferous, deep forest. Its form and coloration (slate-gray upperparts and rusty orange breast) are quite similar to those of the American Robin. It can be distinguished by a

broad black band across its breast, and an orange stripe over the eyes. During winter it seeks the berries of madrone trees. It is not a common garden bird.

Wrentit
(Old World Warbler/ Thrush Family)

Shy and elusive, seldom venturing more than a few feet out of brushy hiding spots, the wrentit is more often heard than seen. Its call is a musical, increasingly rapid trill, with a rhythm similar to the accelerating bounces of a ping-pong ball dropped on a hard surface. The wrentit resembles a cross between a wren and a titmouse, as its head and bill resemble those of the crestless tit, and its long tail, often cocked at a right angle, gray-brown upperparts and cinnamon-brown breast, and active yet secretive habits, are similar to those of wrens.

Habitat: Wrentits live in dense, brushy, and preferably uninterrupted chaparral. They choose their home territory of about 2½ acres, usually near that

of the parents, early in life, and seldom depart from it. Wrentits hop about from bush to bush, and almost never fly across open spaces as large as 30 feet. Gardens with large areas of dense shrubbery, especially native-plant gardens that include chaparral shrubs like manzanita, coyote bush, and ceanothus, are most likely to attract them. Nearby hillsides of natural chaparral and brush are a real plus, as is a source of water located very near shrubby cover.

Nesting: Wrentits build their nests in the dense, twiggy growth of shrubs and small trees, in thickets or solid brush. The small cup nests are constructed of plant fibers and bound with spider webs.

Feeding: Wrentits glean many insects from the bark of shrubs and small trees, but fleshy fruits and berries constitute over half their diet. Poison oak berries are a favorite natural plant food; the fruits of brambles, toyon, elderberry, sumac, and Pacific wax myrtle are also important. Wrentits almost never feed on the ground. They enjoy bread crumbs, but will visit only those feeders that are located close to shrubby cover.

Gray Catbird
(Mockingbird Family)

The Gray Catbird is easily identified by its plain slate-gray coloration with a black cap and a reddish patch under the tail. Its typical call is a catlike mew. It occasionally mimics the calls of other birds, although it is not nearly as accomplished at this art as its close relative the Mockingbird. It is relatively fearless around humans, often coming quite close when its call is imitated.

Habitat: The Gray Catbird inhabits brushy thickets of shrubs and vines, preferably at streamsides and marshy forest edges, but also at roadsides. It frequently resides in gardens, often quite close to houses. In fact, human settlements have greatly expanded the range of this bird by increasing the areas of forest edges.

Nesting: The Gray Catbird's cup nest is generally placed low in a dense shrub, vine, or thicket at the margin of a stream or

marsh, or at a forest edge. Sometimes it is found in a low tree, especially a conifer. Garden shrubs like duetzia, lilac, mock orange, and brambles are frequent nesting sites.

Feeding: About half of the Gray Catbird's diet (less in spring and summer, more in fall and winter) is plant food, the rest being large quantities of insects. Fruits and berries that have fallen to the ground are its favorite plant foods, and the list of fruits it enjoys is very long. Brambles, cherries, holly berries, bayberries, and greenbrier berries are at the top. Gray Catbirds frequent the feeding station in spring and summer for dried berries, chopped fresh fruits, cheese, peanut kernels, and bread and cracker crumbs.

Northern Mockingbird
(Mockingbird Family)

The Northern Mockingbird—formerly called simply Mockingbird—is easy to identify by its gray color, long tail, and white wing patches flashing in flight. It is one of the most popular songbirds, famous for its expert mimicry of

Brown Thrasher

Cedar Waxwing

many other birds and mechanical noises, but its tendency to sing loudest and longest on moonlit nights can be very disturbing to sleepers.

Habitat: Prime habitats for this bird include the edges of woods bordering open country, and fields and meadows with isolated shrubby thickets and groves of trees. Its three main habitat requirements are open grassy ground for insect foraging, dense shrubs for nesting, and a high perch for singing and proclaiming its territory. Gardens are among its favorite dwelling places, especially if there are winter berries. Mockingbirds are vigorously territorial, both for summer breeding and winter feeding rights. Most are nonmigratory, permanent residents.
Nesting: Cup nests are constructed in crotches or among the dense twigs of shrubs, low trees, or vines, usually about 5 to 10 feet above the ground. Low coniferous or broad-leafed evergreen trees are favorites, as are thorny, dense shrubs like multiflora roses and bayberries. These birds breed from March to August.
Feeding: About 60 percent of the Northern Mockingbird's diet consists of

animal food, mostly insects. While foraging in grassy areas for grasshoppers and beetles (its most important insect foods), the Mockingbird frequently hitches its wings back and up, possibly to flush insects into view. Plant foods include a wide range of fruits and berries: holly, Virginia creeper, hackberry, brambles, pyracantha, cotoneaster, grapes, and figs are among the most important, but represent only a fraction of the complete list. Mockingbirds visit feeding stations in summer and winter for suet, bread crumbs, and chopped dried fruit, especially raisins.

Brown Thrasher
(Mockingbird Family)

This shy, secretive bird sometimes nests in gardens. Also called *Brown Mockingbird*, it is sometimes confused with thrushes, but is distinguished by a longer tail, a larger body, rufous upperparts, and streaked, not mottled, underparts. It occasionally mimics other birds and mechanical noises, whistling in short, staccato bursts.

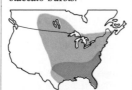

Habitat: Thickets and dry brushy patches in old

fields, woodland edges, and roadsides are likely places to find the Brown Thrasher. It sometimes nests in gardens that have large, dense patches of shrubs and hedges.
Nesting: Low, thorny shrubs and low-branching prickly trees are favorite nesting spots for this bird. Smilax, gooseberry, hawthorn, honey locust, wild plum, and barberry are typical nesting plants. The large, basketlike nest may even be placed directly on the ground. Brown Thrashers breed from March to July.
Feeding: Brown Thrashers forage mostly on the ground, picking up and tossing aside leaves and other debris to look for insects, grubs, fruits, and seeds. Many fruits and berries are important foods, especially in winter, including blackberries, wild cherries, elderberries, dogwood berries, blueberries, bayberries, and grapes. Waste corn and wheat are also eaten. Brown Thrashers in many areas come readily to feeding stations. Scratch feed, cracked corn, and millet are favorite foods, along with bread crumbs, suet and suet mixtures, raisins, and oranges. They prefer ground feeding, but may occasionally be enticed onto platform feeders.

Cedar Waxwing
(Waxwing Family)

This beautiful, crested bird is most readily identified by its gray-brown color, contrasting black mask across the eyes, usually bright red, waxy wingtips, and yellow belly and tail band. They often travel in flocks of 40 or more during the nonbreeding season. The Bohemian Waxwing, a larger but quite similar Canadian bird that occasionally moves down to the northern United States when food is scarce, differs in having a rusty under-tail area and otherwise gray underparts.

Habitat: Waxwings rove quite a bit, and may appear anywhere there are abundant fleshy fruits on trees and shrubs. Their favorite habitats in the nonbreeding season include orchards, parks, forest edges, and second-growth woodlands along streams and rivers. In the breeding season, pairs seek out nesting territories near farm ponds and open woodlands.
Nesting: These birds are gregarious by nature, and sometimes nest in loose

colonies of a dozen or so pairs. They readily use wool, string, hair, and other materials set out by humans. Their cup nests are placed in trees in a wide variety of situations. They usually breed late in the summer, from July to September, but sometimes as early as June.
Feeding: About 90 percent of the Cedar Waxwing's diet consists of fleshy fruits and berries, both wild and cultivated. When a flock descends on a tree or shrubby patch laden with fruit they tend to gorge themselves heavily. Juniper berries are a favorite food, followed closely by European mountain ash, pyracantha, cotoneaster, cherries, dogwood, mistletoe, privet, apple, toyon, hawthorn, Russian olive, California peppertree, grapes, and strawberries. Adults feed the young nestlings with insects, which they hunt in the air like flycatchers. These birds are difficult to entice to the bird feeder; but once they notice it, they will consume large amounts of raisins, currants, and chopped or sliced apples. The best way to attract Cedar Waxwings to your garden, besides planting abundant fruit trees and shrubs, is to provide a birdbath. Like most fruit-eating birds, they get quite thirsty.

European Starling

White-eyed Vireo

Warbling Vireo

European Starling
(Starling Family)

The European Starling is a glossy black bird with a metallic sheen, speckled with light spots in winter. It is included here not to explain how to attract it, but how to repel it. First introduced to New York's Central Park in 1890, it has spread prolifically to all parts of the country. Its consumption of enormous quantities of harmful insects is a benefit to humans, but it also eats fruits and grain crops, and is a serious competitor with many native birds such as Northern Flickers, Great Crested Flycatchers, and bluebirds for nesting cavities.

Habitat: Starlings prefer open country, including farmlands, orchards, and urban and suburban areas. They avoid woodlands, but are extremely adaptable to a wide variety of habitats. Thousands of individuals roost communally, especially in fall and winter, in buildings and trees.
Nesting: This bird is a cavity-nester, and competes aggressively with many native songbirds and woodpeckers for nesting sites. Starlings can't invade nesting boxes with entrance holes smaller than 2 inches, but unfortunately this also excludes several larger birds, especially the Northern Flicker.
Feeding: Starlings invade feeders and bird baths in large flocks, driving away other birds and consuming large quantities of food. Because they prefer to feed on the ground, and are quite wary of humans, establishing a special feeding area far from the house, stocked with cheaper foods they favor, can divert them from feeders intended for more desirable species. Stocking feeders with foods that starlings won't eat is also an effective tactic. They are especially fond of suet, bakery crumbs, peanut hearts, hulled oats, kitchen scraps of all kinds, cracked corn, chicken feed, cooked rice and corn, and canned and soaked dry dog food. They avoid sunflower seeds, whole-kernel corn, hardened suet, thistle, buckwheat, and peanuts in the shell.

White-eyed Vireo
(Vireo Family)

This little warblerlike bird can be identified by yellow face markings frequently described as "spectacles," bright white eyes, and yellow flanks. It frequently surprises intruders with a loud explosive whistle unexpected for its small size. It is apt to nest in gardens.

Habitat: Unlike other vireos, which usually favor tall trees, the White-eyed Vireo inhabits the thorny, brushy thickets of moist lowlands, drier hillsides and old fields, and forest openings and edges. Large dense stands of blackberry, multiflora and other shrubby roses, shrubby willows, dogwoods, and plums encourage its presence in the garden. Dense shrub beds and thick stands of young saplings are best, especially when they adjoin a deeper woodland.
Nesting: White-eyed Vireos suspend their deeply cupped nests from the forks of twigs on the ends of shrub or sapling branches, usually close to the edge of woods. Like all vireos, their nests are marvels of construction, of soft plant fibers, down, rootlets, grasses, and the like carefully woven together, bound with spider webs, and camouflaged on the outside with moss and lichen. White-eyed Vireos breed from March to July.

Feeding: Although it feeds primarily on insects captured on or near the ground, the White-eyed Vireo eats more fruits and berries than is usual in the family; as much as 30 percent of its diet in fall consists of plant food, although the proportion is much less in other seasons. Southern wax myrtle, mulberries, dogwood, and wild grapes are the most important source of plant food, but blackberries, elderberries, and the fruits of holly and Virginia creeper are also eaten. It seldom if ever visits the feeding station.
Related Species: Bell's Vireo is the western counterpart of the White-eyed Vireo. It is a small, rather nondescript bird easily confused with kinglets and the Warbling Vireo. It nests in gardens less frequently than its eastern cousin. Brushy thickets, forest edges, washes, and ravines are its favored habitats.

Warbling Vireo
(Vireo Family)

This is a plain-looking bird, a dull olive-gray above and lighter below, without the red eye and boldly white-bordered crown of the Red-eyed Vireo. Its constant musical song is the essence of summer. It frequently nests in gardens and parks, but is not as plentiful in the East as the Red-eyed Vireo.

Habitat: This bird prefers groves of trees like elms, sycamores, alders, maples, and cottonwoods along streams and rivers. Other likely dwellings are isolated trees and groves in drier uplands, and desert ravines. The most attractive garden habitats are those with large deciduous trees.
Nesting: Like the Red-eyed Vireo, the Warbling Vireo hangs a pendant, cuplike nest on the outermost forks of twigs. It is usually found much higher in the tree than the nests of other vireos, from 30 to 60 feet up. Occasionally the nest is placed quite low, from 5 to 15 feet, in a small tree, sapling, or shrub.
Feeding: Warbling Vireos live almost exclusively on insects, especially caterpillars, that they pick off foliage and twigs. They also occasionally eat dogwood berries and elderberries. Since they migrate to Central America for winter, they do not visit winter feeding stations.

Red-eyed Vireo

Yellow Warbler

Yellow-rumped Warbler

Red-eyed Vireo
(Vireo Family)

Long considered one of the most populous songbirds in eastern North America, this active, constantly singing vireo has suffered some recent population declines. This small, greenish gray bird is distinguished from the similar Warbling Vireo by its bright red eyes, gray crown, and white striped eyebrow. It migrates to Central and South America for the winter. It is seen in gardens only during the summer, or on migration.

Habitat: Red-eyed Vireos can be found nearly anywhere that there are deciduous trees within its range. Open woods, forest clearings and edges, and groves of trees in open country, and dense stands of young saplings under a more mature canopy, are also prime dwelling spots.
Nesting: The Red-eyed Vireo hangs it tiny cup nest from a twig at the end of a branch, or from a low tree limb. The breeding season is from May to August.
Feeding: In spring the Red-eyed Vireo feeds almost exclusively on insects it gleans from the twigs and foliage of trees. The proportion of plant food it eats rises gradually to about 25 percent just before fall migration. Berries are its most important plant food, including those of serviceberry, mulberry, dogwood, Virginia creeper, spicebush, elderberry, blackberry, and tupelo. They also eat cherries, and the seeds of sumac, magnolia, and sassafras.

Yellow Warbler
(Wood Warbler Subfamily)

The cheery song and bright yellow coloration of the male Yellow Warbler make it a welcome visitor to many gardens. The male is distinguished from other yellow birds by the chestnut stripes on his breast. The female is an almost uniform lemon yellow, and immature birds are olive green. Often seen in breeding season and during migration, this warbler winters in Mexico and south to Peru and Brazil.

Habitat: The preferred nesting habitats of this bird are lowland thickets of alder, willow, elderberry, elm saplings, box elder, or dogwood bordering streams and moist lowlands. Woodland edges, forest clearings of shrubby second growth, roadside hedges, fencerows, and patches of trees and shrubs in more open country are also favored spots. In the garden, hedges and shrub borders backed by trees on one side and open lawn and flower beds on the other are good nesting spots.
Nesting: The Yellow Warbler often weaves its cup nest in the upright fork of a low shrub in a thicket, about 6 or 7 feet above the ground; but if tall streamside or floodplain trees, especially willows and cottonwoods, are available it may nest as high as 60 feet. Sunny woodland openings and edges are first choices for nesting. Yellow Warblers breed from April to July.
Feeding: Virtually the entire diet of Yellow Warblers consists of insects, especially caterpillars and other insect larvae. They rarely if ever visit feeding stations.

Yellow-rumped Warbler
(Wood Warbler Subfamily)

Formerly considered two species, the western Audubon's Warbler and the eastern Myrtle Warbler have been found to breed freely where their ranges meet, so both are now officially known as the Yellow-rumped Warbler. This is the most common warbler to visit winter feeding stations. The western subspecies has a yellow throat, and the eastern one has a white throat; both are distinguished from other warblers by their bright yellow rump.

Habitat: Yellow-rumped Warblers nest in the coniferous forests of mountains in the far North, and seem to prefer the edges of mature forests where conifers like firs and spruces mix with deciduous trees. They are more likely to be seen in gardens in winter, when their habitat requirements are less specific, and they rove about quite a bit. In winter this bird may visit any kind of woodland or grove of trees, as well as open fields and shrubby hillsides.
Nesting: Yellow-rumped Warblers often build their nests on the horizontal limbs of tall conifers, especially pines, up to 50 feet above the ground. Sometimes they nest in deciduous trees, or even in low thorny shrubs. They breed from April to July.
Feeding: The Yellow-rumped Warbler feeds mainly on insects, catching them on the wing or plucking them off of twigs and foliage. Compared to other warblers, they eat quite a

Scarlet Tanager

Rose-breasted Grosbeak

Northern Cardinal

few berries in fall and winter, which explains their ability to survive farther North in winter. Bayberries and juniper berries are their staple winter foods in the East, along with the fruits of dogwood, Virginia creeper, poison ivy, and palmetto. In the West, favorites include poison oak, figs, laurel sumac, elderberries, grapes, and Pacific wax myrtle. Yellow-rumped Warblers may need a little coaxing to discover a feeder in winter; branches of their wild foods can alert them to your efforts. Once discovered, your feeder is likely to be visited regularly by more than one of these birds. Along with millet and other seeds, raisins and grape jelly are favorite winter foods, as are suet, peanut butter mix, and bakery crumbs.

Scarlet Tanager
(Tanager Subfamily)

The bright scarlet body with black wings and tail of the male Scarlet Tanager are distinctive; the female is yellow-olive. Shy and difficult to detect when lurking in its usual spot high in the treetops, this brilliantly colored bird may occasionally be enticed to bird feeders.

Habitat: Scarlet Tanagers are forest birds, preferring dense, mature forests. Tall oaks, tulip trees, hickories, ashes, pines, and hemlocks are their favorite trees. Gardens with a dense

woodland habitat or mature forests close by are most likely to attract these birds, which visit gardens only occasionally. They migrate to South America for the winter.

Nesting: The Scarlet Tanager's nest is a shallow cup of twigs, pine needles, and fibrous plant material resting on a horizontal branch of a deciduous tree, generally well out from the trunk and up to 75 feet above the ground. Oaks are among its favored nesting trees. The breeding season is from May to August.

Feeding: Tanagers are mostly insect-eaters, but do eat fleshy fruits. Serviceberries, mulberries, blueberries, brambles, and grapes are among their favorite garden plants. They occasionally visit summer feeders for sliced apples, oranges, and bananas; raisins; bakery crumbs; and peanut butter mix. These birds spend most of their time feeding high in treetops, but they also forage in shrubs and on the ground. They prefer second-story window feeders and platform feeders raised high off the ground, but they can be persuaded to use lower feeding stations, even those on the ground.

Related Species: The Summer Tanager is the southern counterpart of the Scarlet Tanager. It naturally inhabits the more open, dry, oak and pine woodlands of the South,

and cottonwood and willow thickets along streams. It is less shy about residing in gardens with open lawns and flower beds bordered by trees and shrub borders. From a distance it may be confused with the Northern Cardinal, but tanagers have no crest, and the solid red color of the Summer Tanager is much rosier. Summer feeding recommendations are the same as for the Scarlet Tanager. Dogwoods, mulberries, tupelo, cherries, and brambles attract it to the garden. It can become quite tame once it learns to use the feeder.

Northern Cardinal
(Cardinal Subfamily)

Possibly the most popular and well-known bird in the East, the male Northern Cardinal is unmistakable for its brilliant red color and crested head. It commonly nests in gardens, and is a frequent visitor to the winter feeding station.

Habitat: Dense thickets and, in the Southwest, mesquite thickets and mixed woodland margins along washes and streams, are the favored habitats of the Northern Cardinal. Canebrakes of brambles and the thickets of open woods, forest edges, and

the borders of fields are also likely spots to find them. In the garden, hedge and shrub borders adjacent to open lawn or drives, backed by a mix of coniferous and deciduous trees, are frequently nest sites.

Nesting: Cardinals build cup nests firmly attached to the forks of small branches in thickets or vines 2 to 12 feet off the ground, or in dense thickets of young saplings. Honeysuckle thickets and young evergreens, as well as dense tangles of thorny shrubs like roses, barberries, and hollies, are favorite garden nesting sites. Cardinals breed from March through August. They are nonmigratory, and select a year-round home range early in life, sometimes not far from their parents. They vigorously defend the breeding territory within this range against other cardinals throughout the breeding and nesting season. The resident pair, and possibly a few young, will visit the summer feeder; winter feeders may host as many as a dozen pairs.

Feeding: For a seed-eating bird, cardinals eat remarkable numbers of insects, especially during the breeding season. They are known to eat over a hundred kinds of fruits and seeds in the wild. Attractive garden plants include brambles, sumac, cherry, dogwood, grape, mulberry, blueberry, elderberry, tulip tree, hackberry, and Russian olive. Many of these plants are also used for

Indigo Bunting

Rufous-sided Towhee

nesting. Cardinals are popular at feeding stations, where they strongly prefer unhulled sunflower seeds over all other foods. When birdseed is offered as a mixture, visiting cardinals are likely to scratch all other seeds on the ground to find all the sunflower seeds. They also eat safflower seeds, white proso millet, bread, nutmeats, and peanut butter mix when sunflower seeds aren't available.

Rose-breasted Grosbeak
(Cardinal Subfamily)

Its striking coloration and fondness for nesting in gardens make this species popular in the Midwest and Northeast. The male is a plump, starling-sized bird with a black head and upperparts, snowy white underparts, wingbars, and bill, and a large, bright, rosy red triangular patch on the breast and under the wings. Most Rose-breasted Grosbeaks spend the winter in Mexico to South America, although a very few remain in the United States. They arrive back at their breeding grounds in early May.

Habitat: Like so many garden birds, Rose-breasted Grosbeaks prefer the thickets of saplings and shrubs where deciduous forests open onto rivers, streams, swamps, pastures, clearings, and old fields. They take to overgrown orchards, and frequently nest in the gardens of towns and suburbs. Gardens especially attractive to them have abundant water, dense plantings of small trees, shrub borders, hedges, and a perimeter of more mature woodland.
Nesting: The loosely woven nest of the Rose-breasted Grosbeak is usually located close to water in a thicket of shrubs or saplings, especially alders or young oaks, in a branch crotch 8 to 20 feet above the ground. Horsehairs are acceptable nesting material to offer them. They breed from May to July.
Feeding: Rose-breasted Grosbeaks eat large numbers of harmful insects, and are a boon around the garden or orchard. Their favorite foods include beetles (especially potato beetles), grasshoppers, and caterpillars. About 40 percent of their diet in spring and summer consists of plant foods, mostly seeds and flower buds foraged in the tops of trees, especially elms, hickories, and beeches. They also eat the seeds and pits of fruits, especially elderberry and wild cherry. Unfortunately, they are especially fond of garden peas. At the summer feeder and especially before migration in the fall they greatly appreciate sunflower seeds. Water for drinking will also attract them.

Indigo Bunting
(Cardinal Subfamily)

In the sunlight the plumage of this bird is a deep, brilliant blue, but in shade it may appear black. Indigo Buntings are sometimes confused with the more rarely seen Blue Grosbeak, but the latter is larger, with a heavier bill and broad brown wingbars. Indigo Buntings are most frequently seen at spring, summer, and fall feeding stations, as they migrate to Central and South America for the winter. Occasionally they may remain year round in Florida, and more rarely farther north.

Habitat: Indigo Buntings live in open, brushy fields and pastures, forest edges, and brushy clearings. They also favor thickets along the margins of rivers and streams. They occasionally nest in gardens that have dense stands of shrubs and hedges, but tend to live in more outlying suburban and rural areas.
Nesting: Dense stands of young saplings and thickets of shrubs, especially thorny canebrakes of raspberries and blackberries, are prime spots for the Indigo Bunting's nest, a cup tightly woven of plant fibers, hair, bits of paper, and even snakeskins. These buntings breed from May to August.
Feeding: Buntings are basically seed-eaters, and are especially fond of the seeds of thistle, goldenrod, aster, grasses, and grains. They also eat insects captured in trees and shrubs or on the ground. Millet and canary seed are favorite foods at feeding stations, but they also eat nutmeats and occasionally fruits. They prefer to feed on the ground, but can be persuaded onto low platforms and even hanging feeders.

Rufous-sided Towhee
(American Sparrow Subfamily)

This colorful towhee is an asset in the garden for its cheerful music and appearance. The black hood, wings, and back and the white-edged tail of the male contrast dramatically with its bright reddish brown flanks and white belly. The western type has white bars and stripes on the wings.

Habitat: The favorite residences of this towhee are shrubby forest edges, thickets, and old fields. In the West they are found in chaparral and juniper-pinyon woodlands and along streams. In the garden, look for them in dense shrubby thickets and hedges, especially evergreen shrubs and brushpiles. These birds frequently reside in suitable gardens the year round.
Nesting: These birds prefer to nest on the ground or close to it, under the cover of a shrub or brush pile. When suitable cover is available, they sometimes nest higher up in a shrub, vine, or low tree. They breed from April to August.
Feeding: Rufous-sided Towhees scratch furiously at leaves and litter as they forage on the ground, usually under the cover of a shrub. Seeds are their primary food, although insects compose nearly half of their diet in spring and summer. Favorite garden food plants include serviceberry, elderberry, and blueberry. These birds will visit summer feeders as well as winter ones, and are partial to sunflower seeds, canary seeds, thistle seeds, millet, finely cracked corn, and suet. They prefer feeding on the ground under a feeder, close to cover, and it is generally best to keep them there. When they alight on elevated feeders their furious scratching sends seeds flying in all directions.

Brown Towhee

American Tree Sparrow

Chipping Sparrow

Brown Towhee
(American Sparrow Subfamily)

This rather plain-looking bird, of a uniform dusty brown with a reddish patch under the tail, is a common resident of gardens in California and the Southwest. It lurks about under shrubs, parked cars, and other suitable cover, emerging to feed on lawns or pavement or under feeders. It often shows little fear of humans. This is surprising, since in the wild this bird is very timid. Even when it is not in sight, however, its frequently pronounced territorial call, a sharp, metallic "chink," alerts us to its presence.

Habitat: Preferred habitats of the Brown Towhee include low shrub in chaparral, streamsides, pinyon, juniper woodlands, and washes in cactus country. Gardens with plenty of dense, low shrubs are very attractive to this bird.
Nesting: The Brown Towhee usually places its cup nest in the densest part of a twiggy shrub or low tree, from 3 to 12 feet above the ground. Animal hair is a suitable nesting material to offer.
Feeding: This bird is a ground feeder, scratching for the seeds of weeds and grasses under shrubs and in dense grassy patches. It often comes to bird feeders for small seeds, especially hulled oats, millet, finely cracked corn, and thistle seed.

American Tree Sparrow
(American Sparrow Subfamily)

Along with the White-throated Sparrow, this is the most common true sparrow to visit winter feeding stations in the Northeast. The American Tree Sparrow can be distinguished from others by the dark brown spot in the center of its plain whitish-gray breast. It has a reddish brown cap. In spring and summer it retires to the northern tundra to breed. The name is misleading, as it spends little time in trees.

Habitat: In winter, small flocks roam about weedy fields, marshes, roadsides, and forest edges. Open lawn and large flower beds gone to seed are the best places to feed this bird in winter.
Nesting: American Tree Sparrows leave the northern states for their Arctic breeding grounds in late March and April. They nest in brushy thickets of willow and other shrubs at the treeline in Alaska and northern Canada.
Feeding: These birds generally eat on the ground in the wild, vigorously scratching for the weed seeds that compose most of their diet. They may also cling to weed tops, pecking for seeds. At feeding stations they can be fed either on the ground or on low platforms. White and red proso millet and finely cracked corn are their preferred foods. They will sometimes eat canary seed and, to a lesser extent, black-striped sunflower seed. Like juncos, American Tree Sparrows are most apt to visit the garden during the harshest, most snowy weather.

Chipping Sparrow
(American Sparrow Subfamily)

Similar to the American Tree Sparrow, this slightly smaller bird has a reddish brown cap, brown-streaked upper parts, and whitish gray underside, but no dark brown spot on the breast. It is most frequently seen in most of North America in spring and summer, and in the southeastern states at winter feeding stations. Chipping Sparrows are shy around other birds, and are frequently driven away from feeders, but they are surprisingly tame around humans.

Habitat: Grassy woodland clearings and edges, and the border of meadows, streams, lakes, and ponds are the preferred habitats of the Chipping Sparrow. An open lawn, bordered by dense flower beds, and with a perimeter of trees, makes a fine garden habitat.
Nesting: The Chipping Sparrow generally builds its cup nest on the limb of a conifer, sometimes as low as 1 foot from the ground, but more often higher up, to 50 feet. Deciduous trees, shrubs, and vines may also be used, and bayberries are a preferred nesting site.
Feeding: In spring and summer over 60 percent of this sparrow's diet consists of insects, especially grasshoppers, caterpillars, and beetles. They eat grass seeds and small weed seeds in great quantities, especially in fall and winter. At southern winter feeders millet and canary seed are especially popular, along with bakery crumbs. Sunflower seeds may occasionally be eaten. To decrease the effects of competition on this non-aggressive bird, broadcast food over a wide area on the ground. When no other birds are around, they will occasionally hop onto low platform feeders.

White-throated Sparrow

White-crowned Sparrow

Song Sparrow

Song Sparrow
(American Sparrow Subfamily)

The bright, cheerful song of this well-named species is a welcome asset in the garden. The dark central breast spot, on white underparts heavily streaked with brown, is a key to distinguishing this highly variable bird from other sparrows. In many parts of its range it may be a permanent resident, but in the deep South it is known only as a winter visitor.

Habitat: This bird favors brushy thickets near water in both summer and winter. Other frequent habitations include drier areas along fencerows, old fields, roadsides, and open groves with dense undergrowth in the plains states. In the garden, brushpiles and dense patches of shrubs next to flower beds are appropriate habitats. A source of water nearby is appreciated, as this bird loves to bathe and drink frequently. Higher perches from which to sing are essential to the male during the breeding season.

Nesting: The first brood each season is raised in neat cups woven of grass and hidden in a weedy patch on or close to the ground. For the next one or two broods, the nest is often built about 4 feet from the ground in a low shrub or tree, especially barberry, but also red cedar, alder, or yew, or in a brushpile. Song sparrows can occasionally be enticed to use special nesting shelves built to the appropriate dimensions and mounted on the wall of a shed, or even the house, 2 to 4 feet from the ground, and behind dense shrubbery. They breed from February to August.

Feeding: These birds eat mostly the small seeds of weeds and grasses, especially in fall and winter. In spring and summer as much as half of their diet may be insects, for which they forage in grassy weed patches and shrubby growth. Winter residents are frequent visitors to the feeding station, especially for millet, canary seed, and finely cracked corn. They prefer eating on the ground, although they often visit elevated feeders.

White-throated Sparrow
(American Sparrow Subfamily)

Sometimes confused with the similar White-crowned Sparrow, this familiar visitor to winter feeders in the East is distinguished by the prominent white patch on its throat and the yellow spot between the eyes and the bill. It is especially loved for its beautiful song, which it often performs in winter.

Habitat: In winter this sparrow prefers brushy streamsides, where it scratches for the seeds of weeds and grasses. It summers in the openings and edges of coniferous and mixed woodlands of the extreme northeastern United States and in Canada. In the garden, ideal spots include dense patches of shrubbery and hedges next to open, grassy areas.

Nesting: White-throated Sparrows raise their young in a grassy cup nest on or near the ground, under dense thickets, at the margins of woods in the North. They breed from May to August.

Feeding: This sparrow comes only rarely to elevated feeders, preferring to feed on the ground near the close cover of shrubs. In the wild, it feeds primarily on small weed seeds. At the feeder, its tastes are similar to those of the White-crowned Sparrow, although it takes more readily to finely cracked corn, enjoying it almost as much as red proso millet. Its favorite foods are hulled sunflower seeds and kernels (often gleaned from the shells left by other birds), and white proso millet.

White-crowned Sparrow
(American Sparrow Subfamily)

The striking black and white stripes on its crown make this bird one of the handsomest sparrows to visit the garden. Although sometimes thought of as a western bird, many individuals also occur in the eastern United States in winter, where they frequently visit feeders.

Habitat: The favorite nesting spots of the White-crowned Sparrow are brushy thickets at the edges of forests, bordering streams, ponds, marshes, and other watery places. Gardens with good shrub cover are especially appropriate for this bird, in both summer and winter.

Nesting: The White-crowned Sparrow usually builds its grassy cup nest on or near the ground, in a patch of grasses and weeds, under a shrub. Sometimes it nests in small conifers or small, twiggy, deciduous trees up to 25 feet above the ground. Grassy open places and shrubby cover are this sparrow's two nesting essentials. The breeding season is from April to August.

Feeding: The small seeds of weeds and grasses are the mainstays of this bird's diet. In late spring and summer they also eat a wide variety of insects. They prefer ground feeding at winter feeding stations, and are easily driven off by more aggressive birds. Peanut kernels and hulled sunflower seeds are its favorite foods, but white proso millet is almost as popular, followed by oil-type and black-striped sunflower seeds, peanut hearts, red proso millet, German millet, canary seed, flax, milo, and finely cracked corn.

Dark-eyed Junco

Red-winged Blackbird

Common Grackle

Dark-eyed Junco
(American Sparrow Subfamily)

Until recently the White-winged Junco, Oregon Junco, and Slate-colored Junco were considered to be separate species. However, since all these species interbreed freely where their ranges overlap, they are now considered to be one species, called the Dark-eyed Junco. If you live in the coniferous forests of the far northern or mountainous United States, a pair of these birds may nest in your garden. Elsewhere these familiar birds are winter visitors. They are mantled with black or sooty gray "ponchos," and their white underparts are sharply defined. Flocks of them are common on the ground under feeders in winter.

Habitat: Juncos nest in the coniferous or mixed forests of the mountains, northern United States and Canada. They prefer the edge of woods bordering a stream, pond, lake, trail, or mountain meadow. Woodland roadsides and the edges of cutover clearings are also attractive. In winter they migrate south or to lower elevations, and roam about in flocks. Forest edges and brushy fields are their favorite winter haunts, along with roadsides, hedges, parks, and gardens. Open ground and flower beds gone to seed are favorite garden attractions, especially if backed by a woodland.
Nesting: Juncos build a grassy nest on or near the ground at a forest edge, preferably close to water, or in a forest with dense ground cover. They breed from late March to August.
Feeding: Most of the Dark-eyed Junco's diet consists of weed seeds, but in the spring and summer they also eat a large number of insects, or feed them to their young. They have a strong preference for ground feeding, but may occasionally alight on low platform feeders. Because they are most common at backyard feeders during bad weather, they are often called *snowbirds*. Red proso millet is their favorite food at winter feeders, followed by white proso millet, canary seed, finely cracked corn, and oil-type sunflower seeds. Suet, peanut butter mix, and peanut hearts are also attractive.

Red-winged Blackbird
(Troupial Subfamily)

The bright red epaulets on the wings of the male of this blackbird are a familiar sight throughout the country in wetlands, farmlands, and brushy fields. Winter feeding stations in the South, and increasingly in the northern states, are often visited by this blackbird. As it travels in huge flocks during the non-breeding seasons, its visits to the average garden feeder can be overwhelming.

Habitat: Red-winged Blackbirds breed in wetlands of many kinds, especially those with thick stands of cattails. They also nest in nearby upland brushy fields and pastures, and forage in flocks in upland fields. During non-breeding seasons they roam the countryside in flocks, visiting all kinds of open land.

Nesting: Red-winged Blackbirds prefer to build their woven cup nests in thick stands of cattails, but shrubs, trees, and grasslands may be used, even if not located next to water. Sometimes they nest solitarily; more often many nests occupy a swamp, marsh, or field at well-spaced intervals. Although extremely territorial on their breeding grounds, these birds feed in flocks.
Feeding: These birds feed on the ground, usually in large flocks. About 75 percent of their diet is plant food, varying from 60 percent in summer to 100 percent in winter. They do eat some grain (mostly waste grain) in farmlands, but they also consume huge quantities of destructive insects. At the bird feeder they devour nearly all kinds of seeds, grains, and nutmeats. They prefer feeding on the ground, but have learned to use all kinds of feeders, even hanging suet feeders. They follow a sporadic schedule; for no apparent reason a large flock may disappear as quickly as it arrived. If you are troubled by large numbers of Red-winged Blackbirds regularly, you may wish to establish a separate feeding area for them on the ground farther from the house.

Common Grackle
(Troupial Subfamily)

Even when nesting in the tall suburban and urban conifers it favors, the Common Grackle is a gregarious bird, preferring close neighbors of its own kind. In the nonbreeding season these large black birds, with a metallic bronze, green, or purple sheen and bright yellow eyes, forage and roost in large flocks, often in the company of cowbirds, starlings, Red-winged Blackbirds, and robins.

Habitat: Before humans came on the scene, Common Grackles favored wet, open woods of lowlands and the borders of marshes. They have adapted readily to human settlements, and can be found in a wide variety of urban and suburban situations, from

Orchard Oriole

Northern Oriole

Purple Finch

parks and "green zones" in cities, to lawns and gardens in the suburbs, and especially in the fields and woodlots of agricultural areas.

Nesting: Common Grackles often erect their massive stick nests in colonies. They favor tall, dense evergreens, but may nest in anything from a low shrub, a hole in a tree or stump, or an old building, to tall deciduous trees. They breed from March to June.

Feeding: Omnivorous and adaptable in feeding, the Common Grackle generally forages for food on the ground, occasionally flying up to snap insects from the air, but it also can feed while wading in water or hopping around in trees and shrubs. It eats virtually anything, from insects, earthworms, and grubs to the eggs and young of other birds, adult small songbirds (especially House Sparrows), mice, frogs, small fish, garbage, and large quantities of seeds, nuts, grains, fruits, and berries. At the bird feeder, sunflower seeds and corn are its favorite foods, along with bakery crumbs and kitchen scraps. Scatter these on the ground away from the house to divert winter flocks from your closer feeders.

Orchard Oriole
(Troupial Subfamily)

Similar to a small, bluebird-sized robin, this oriole has a reddish brown breast and body with a black head, back, wings, and tail. It frequently nests in loose colonies in fruit trees, where it destroys many harmful pests.

Habitat: Like the Northern Oriole, the Orchard Oriole frequently nests in trees overhanging rivers and streams. It often lives in orchards, where it finds plentiful insects and the few fruits that it eats, and in shade and street trees in suburban areas.

Nesting: The Orchard Oriole hangs its tightly woven pendulous nest from the tip of a tree branch, sometimes in scattered colonies. It breeds from April to July.

Feeding: More than 90 percent of the Orchard Oriole's diet is insects, although it occasionally eats a few fruits. Mulberries are a favorite, as are brambles, cherries, and blueberries.

Northern Oriole
(Troupial Subfamily)

The Baltimore Oriole of the East and its western counterpart, Bullock's Oriole, are now considered to belong to the same species, recently named Northern Oriole. The males of both subspecies are colorful birds, with a bright orange-yellow body and a black back and wings. The head of the eastern oriole is all black, while the western one has a black crown and eyeline, a narrow black bib, and a broader white stripe on the wings. They commonly interbreed where their ranges overlap. Both have adapted well to living in gardens and suburban areas, and can occasionally be enticed to the summer feeder.

Habitat: The Northern Oriole prefers tall shade trees with shrubby undergrowth, and in the Southwest favors the mesquite groves of desert washes. It can also be found in open woods and oak savannas. This adaptable bird has learned to nest in the gardens and streetsides of suburban areas, especially in ornamental trees like the American elm that derive from floodplain habitats.

Nesting: The Northern Oriole weaves a pendulous, sacklike nest that hangs from the branch tips of tall trees, often over a river, street, or drive. Offering horse hair, string, and other nesting material in pieces no longer than 8 inches will help entice these birds to nest nearby. Elms and maples are favorite nesting trees.

Feeding: Northern Orioles eat primarily insects, but in summer and fall as much as 20 percent of their diet may be fleshy fruits and berries. Mulberries, serviceberries, brambles, cherries, mountain ash, nuts, and figs are among their favorite plant foods. Chopped fruit, and fruits like pears, apples, and oranges halved and firmly attached to a platform feeder, will attract them. They also enjoy jelly, especially grape and apple. They will visit hummingbird feeders if there is enough of a perch. Although migratory, the Northern Oriole has been staying north in winter in increasing numbers.

Purple Finch
(Finch Family)

The Purple Finch is difficult to distinguish from its close relative the House Finch, but the male has a darker, more uniform rosy or wine coloration that is not as concentrated on the head and breast. It is a frequent visitor to feeding stations in winter, and often breeds in summer gardens.

Habitat: The Purple Finch breeds in northern coniferous or mixed coniferous-deciduous forests, especially around the openings of swamps, streams, and logged-over clearings. At breeding time it is likely to be attracted to a group of conifers, especially firs and spruces, at the edge of a garden woodland, particularly if water is available. In the winter Purple Finches usually travel in flocks about a

House Finch

Pine Siskin

American Goldfinch

wide range of habitats.
Nesting: Purple Finches build their shallow cup nest well out on the limb of a conifer, frequently as high as 60 feet above the ground. Firs, spruces, pines, and redwoods are popular residences; box-elder, ash, and dogwood may also be used. The breeding season is from April to July.
Feeding: Purple Finches are almost entirely vegetarian, although they may feed a few beetles and caterpillars to their young. Buds (including, unfortunately, the flower buds of many fruit trees), soft fruits, and seeds form most of their diet. Favorite food plants in the garden include fir, maple, birch, ash, juniper, sweet gum, tupelo, mulberry, dogwood, and pyracantha. At bird feeders they are fond of sunflower seeds, especially the oil-type, and, to a lesser extent, feed on canary seed and thistle. They will come to all kinds of feeders, but prefer them high off the ground, like second-story window trays.

House Finch
(Finch Family)

Both in its native western range and in the East (where it was introduced in the 1940s by cage-bird dealers), the House Finch has adapted to human set-

tlements in much the same way as the House Sparrow. It is somewhat less aggressive, however, and has a prettier song and brighter coloration. Although it is often confused with the Purple Finch, the red coloration on the crown, breast, and rump of the male House Finch is normally brighter than the wine colors of the male Purple Finch. The male House Finch can also be distinguished by its brown-streaked flanks.

Habitat: Brushy deserts, chaparral, and old fields are popular dwelling spots for the House Finch. It is widely adapted to areas around buildings.
Nesting: The House Finch is very adaptable in its choice of a nesting site. It frequently chooses cavities, from holes in buildings to tree stumps, old woodpecker holes, and nesting boxes. Or it may nest in a tree, shrub, cactus, vines on buildings, or even on the ground. House Finches are gregarious at all times of the year; they often nest in colonies and travel in flocks in the nonbreeding season.
Feeding: Although House Finches eat a few insects—

mostly fed to the young in spring—nearly all of their diet in summer, fall, and winter consists of plant food. They eat mostly weed seeds, but are fond of soft fruits, which sometimes gets them in trouble in orchards and other agricultural areas. They regularly extract and eat the seeds from winter berries. At western feeding stations just about any type of feeder and any type of food are attractive, including suet, all types of birdseed, most fruits, bakery crumbs, and kitchen scraps. These birds even visit hummingbird feeders. At eastern feeders they confine themselves mainly to birdseed. Sunflower, thistle, white proso millet, and canary seeds are their favorites, in that order.

Pine Siskin
(Finch Family)

Dusky brown streaking all over and yellow markings on the wing and tail help to distinguish this little finch from its relatives. Although it is somewhat uncommon at winter feeders, when it does visit it usually does so in flocks of up to 200 individuals. Siskins apparently use House Sparrows to alert them to feeders, but once siskins discover a food source they often drive the House Sparrows off for the winter. Pine

Siskins are remarkbly tame toward humans.

Habitat: Pine Siskins prefer nesting in the edges of coniferous forests and in logged-over second-growth forest clearings in the mountains and the north. In the winter they roam about in large flocks, and can be found just about anywhere that food is available. They prefer garden habitats resembling woodland edges opening onto grassy areas, and flower beds allowed to go to seed.
Nesting: Often nesting in loose colonies, Pine Siskins build their cup nests on the outer stretches of horizontal conifer limbs about 10 feet above the ground. Pines and hemlocks are frequent choices. They breed from April to July.
Feeding: Pine Siskins typically feed on tall weeds, tearing the seed heads apart, then dropping to the ground to eat them. Seeds of trees, especially alder, birch, spruce, pine, sweet gum, and maple are also favorites. During the summer breeding season they eat many insects, and feed them to their young. Thistle seeds are a favorite at the winter feeder, either in

hanging feeders or scattered on the ground. They also enjoy canary seed, millet, finely cracked corn, sunflower seeds, suet, and nutmeats.

American Goldfinch
(Finch Family)

Bright yellow with a striking black cap, wings, and tail, the male American Goldfinch provides a cheery touch to the garden as it flashes around in its characteristic undulating flight. Duller and browner in the nonbreeding season, it is quite sociable and apt to visit garden feeders in hungry flocks of 30 or so.

Habitat: Weedy fields, orchards, meadows with a few scattered trees, openings in forests, and brushy old fields are favorite haunts of the American Goldfinch. Especially when nesting, they are seldom found far from thistles. In winter they roam about in nearly all types of open terrain. The best way to attract these birds is to provide water, as they love to bathe.
Nesting: Hedges and shrubs near grassy, weedy

Evening Grosbeak

House Sparrow

meadows are preferred nesting sites. The nest is a cup of plant fibers and thistledown woven so tightly that it will hold water. Sometimes it is placed in a small tree, or in a patch of thistles. American Goldfinches breed from late June to September (in California they may start as early as April), when the weed seeds they feed their young begin to ripen.

Feeding: In the spring as much as half of the food these birds forage can be insects, which they feed to their young. At other times virtually all of their diet is vegetarian, principally weed seeds and the hard, dry seeds of trees. Garden food plants include serviceberry, birch, hornbeam, sweet gum, mulberry, hemlock, elm, and alder. At the bird feeder hulled sunflower seeds and pieces are preferred, followed by thistle seed, their most important natural food. They also eat unhulled sunflower seeds, especially the oiltype. Hanging feeders are appropriate for this bird, although they will visit all types of feeders, including ground feeders.

Evening Grosbeak
(Finch Family)

This beautiful garden visitor looks something like a very plump, starling-sized goldfinch, although the yellow coloration of the male

is darker and the olive-green head has a massive, yellow, cone-shaped bill.

Habitat: The Evening Grosbeak prefers dense coniferous and mixed deciduous-coniferous forests for nesting, and also year-round when food is plentiful. However, this bird is expanding into a variety of habitats, possibly because of increased planting of maples, the seeds of which are a preferred food, and especially since the provision of sunflower seeds at winter feeders has become popular. During the nonbreeding season, the highly social Evening Grosbeak is prone to wander in sizable flocks over a variety of habitats. Mature conifers, especially spruces and firs, and mature maples, particularly box elders, make a garden attractive to this bird.

Nesting: Evening Grosbeaks build a shallow cup of twigs that is usually placed at the twiggy end of a conifer branch as high as 70 feet off the ground. They sometimes use deciduous trees such as willow, maple, ash, birch, or oak. They breed from May to July.

Feeding: In summer a

fairly large percentage of this bird's diet consists of insects, but in the other seasons nearly all of its food is vegetable. They especially relish the seeds of maple trees and the fruits of dogwoods; the seeds of pine, spruce, fir, wild cherry, mountain ash, juniper, manzanita, Russian olive, hackberry, snowberry, and serviceberry are also popular. When feeding on fleshy fruits such as crab apples, Evening Grosbeaks usually reject the fleshy part and eat the hard seeds or pits. At the feeder, these birds love sunflower seeds, which a flock will consume in vast quantities on cold days, and they will eat little else. They prefer high platform feeders, like second-story window feeders, but when a large flock arrives it is wise to offer seed over a wider area, on the ground and on other platform feeders, to avoid squabbling. Evening Grosbeaks are attracted to water for drinking, but they have seldom been observed to bathe.

House Sparrow
(Old World Sparrow Family)

This aggressive, highly competitive import, formerly known as the English Sparrow, should not be confused with the native sparrows, which are generally shy, musical grassland

birds. In less than 60 years from their introduction in Brooklyn, New York, in 1850, the House Sparrow had become established in nearly all parts of the populated United States. Although their population has declined somewhat since horses are no longer used so much (undigested oats in manure were a staple of their diet), they can still be bothersome in the bird garden, driving other birds away from feeders and usurping nesting boxes.

Habitat: Almost any place settled by humans is attractive to this highly adaptable bird, including cities, suburbs, and agricultural areas.

Nesting: In North America, House Sparrows are cavity nesters. Nesting boxes and crevices in buildings are their favorite spots. If no cavities are available, they will construct their own: a large, globular mass of grass, straw, and other plant fibers in a tree, with several small openings in the side leading to a "room" inside. House Sparrows will not nest in any birdhouse with an opening of less than 1⅛ inch, but unfortunately this size also excludes almost all desir-

able birds, except for chickadees and House Wrens. These wary birds usually shun birdhouses mounted low on a post, 4 or 5 feet off the ground, and this can be an effective technique for favoring some birds, particularly bluebirds. Martin houses are frequently invaded by the earlier-nesting House Sparrow. To reserve your apartment house for its intended residents, observe when the regularly migrating martins are due to return, and erect the Martin house as close to that time as possible each year.

Feeding: House Sparrows feed largely on plants, although they do eat some insects in the summer. Their winter staples are small seeds and grain picked off the ground. If ground feeding stations are established farther from the house and stocked with favorite House Sparrow foods, these wary birds may be diverted from the closer feeders intended for other guests. White proso millet, bakery crumbs, and kitchen scraps are preferred foods, followed by canary seed, red proso millet, German millet, and sunflower seeds. House Sparrows prefer to eat on the ground, although they will come to platform feeders. They avoid wobbly hanging feeders, and generally will not enter small, closed structures like tin cans.

As Your Interest Grows

You couldn't ask for a safer and more benevolent hobby than attracting birds. About the only "danger" with this pursuit is its addictive nature. One of the best ways to expand your activity is by joining the National Wildlife Federation and participating in their Backyard Wildlife Program. This program is designed for people with property from windowsill size up to three acres. Applicants who agree to provide certain minimum requirements of food, water, and shelter receive a Backyard Wildlife Registration Certificate, in addition to a newsletter and a large list of publications that can be ordered. For further information write to:

Backyard Wildlife Program
National Wildlife Federation
1412 Sixteenth Street, N.W.
Washington, D.C. 20036

A subscription to any of the following publications, newsletters, and magazines will keep you informed regarding techniques of bird attracting and the experiences of other people in this field.

Birding News Survey
Avian Publications, Inc.
P.O. Box 310
Elizabethtown, KY 42701

Bird Watcher's Digest
P.O. Box 110
Marietta, Ohio 45750

The Bird Watch
Bird Populations Institute
P.O. Box 637
Manhattan, KS 66502

Wild Bird Guide
Bird Friends Society
Essex, CT 06426

Nature Society News
Griggsville, IL 62340

Acorn Woodpecker

Before you know it, you may find yourself stalking the wilds beyond your property lines, searching for the bird that just won't come into the yard. Bird watching, listing, and photography are popular activities, and many local clubs and societies, too numerous to list here, sponsor field trips and informative programs. The first place to check is your local chapter of the National Audubon Society. For information on local organizations, write to their national headquarters.

National Audubon Society
950 Third Avenue
New York, NY 10022

Dimensions of Birdhouses

The information in this chart has been adapted from Conservation Bulletin #14 of the U.S. Department of the Interior, Fish and Wildlife Service, *Homes for Birds*. Further information on constructing bird houses can be obtained by ordering this pamphlet from:

**Superintendent of Documents
U.S. Government Printing Office
Washington, D.C. 20402**

The stock number is 024-010-00524-4, and the cost is $2.50.

Bird	Floor of House	Depth of House	Diameter of Entrance Hole	Height of Entrance Above Floor	Height Above Ground
	Dimensions in Inches				*Feet*
American Kestrel	8 x 8	12 to 15	3	9 to 12	10 to 30
Eastern Bluebird	5 x 5	8	1-1/2	6	5 to 10
Carolina Wren	4 x 4	6 to 8	1-1/2	4 to 6	6 to 10
Chickadee	4 x 4	8 to 10	1-1/8	6 to 8	6 to 15
Downy Woodpecker	4 x 4	8 to 10	1-1/4	6 to 8	6 to 20
House Finch	6 x 6	6	2	4	8 to 12
House Wren	4 x 4	6 to 8	1 to 1-1/4	4 to 6	6 to 10
Northern Flicker	7 x 7	16 to 18	2-1/2	14 to 16	6 to 20
Nuthatch	4 x 4	8 to 10	1-1/4	6 to 8	12 to 20
Purple Martin*	6 x 6	6	2-1/2	1	12 to 20
Red-bellied Woodpecker	6 x 6	12 to 15	2-1/2	9 to 12	12 to 20
Red-headed Woodpecker	6 x 6	12 to 15	2	9 to 12	12 to 20
Screech Owl	8 x 8	12 to 15	3	9 to 12	10 to 30
Starling	6 x 6	16 to 18	2	14 to 16	10 to 25
Titmouse	4 x 4	8 to 10	1-1/4	6 to 8	6 to 15
Tree Swallow	5 x 5	6	1-1/2	1 to 5	10 to 15
Winter Wren	4 x 4	6 to 8	1 to 1-1/4	4 to 6	6 to 10
Nesting Shelves					
American Robin	6 x 8	8			6 to 15
Barn Swallow	6 x 6	6			8 to 12
Eastern Phoebe	6 x 6	6			8 to 12
Song Sparrow	6 x 6	6			1 to 3

*Dimensions are for one compartment (one pair of birds); martin houses are usually built eight compartments at a time.

Adapted from *Homes for Birds*, U.S. Department of the Interior, Fish and Wildlife Service.